Conveniently
HOMEMADE
Main Dishes

Printed in the United States of America
by G&R Publishing Company

Distributed by:

 Products

507 Industrial Street
Waverly, IA 50677

ISBN-13: 978-1-56383-240-6
ISBN-10: 1-56383-240-2

Item #7101

Dinner Nachos Supreme

Makes 4 servings

1 lb. ground beef
1 (1¼ oz.) pkg. taco
  seasoning mix
1 (10¾ oz.) can
  tomato soup
1½ C. water
1½ C. instant white rice,
  uncooked

Chunky salsa
Shredded Cheddar
  cheese
Shredded lettuce
Tortilla chips

In a large skillet over medium heat, place ground beef and taco seasoning. Heat, stirring frequently, until ground beef is browned. Pour off fat from browned ground beef and stir in tomato soup, water and instant rice. Bring mixture to a boil, cover and reduce to low heat for 5 minutes, or until rice is thoroughly cooked Remove from heat and transfer mixture to a serving bowl. Top with salsa, shredded Cheddar cheese and shredded lettuce. Serve with tortilla chips for dipping

Quick Herbed Chicken & Seasoned Rice

Makes 4 servings

1 T. vegetable oil
4 boneless chicken
  breast halves
1 (10¾ oz.) can cream
  of chicken soup
½ cup milk

1 (10½ oz.) can
  chicken broth
1 C. water
2 C. instant white rice,
  uncooked

    In a large skillet over medium heat, place vegetable oil and chicken and heat, turning once, until browned on both sides. Add cream of chicken soup and milk to skillet and bring to a boil. Cover and reduce heat to low, simmering for 5 minutes or until chicken is cooked throughout. Meanwhile, to prepare rice, in a small saucepan over medium high heat, place chicken broth and water. Bring to a boil and stir in instant white rice. Remove from heat and cover. Let rice stand for 5 minutes before fluffing with a fork. Serve chicken on a bed of rice.

Garlic Pork Chops

Makes 4 servings

1 T. vegetable oil
4 boneless pork chops
1 clove garlic, minced

1 (10¾ oz.) can cream
   of mushroom soup
½ cup milk

In a large skillet over medium heat, place vegetable oil, pork chops and minced garlic and cook until browned on both sides, turning once. Add cream of mushroom soup and milk to skillet and bring to a boil. Cover skillet and reduce to low heat for 10 minutes, or until heated throughout.

Skillet Stir Fry Beef Pot Pie

Makes 6 to 8 servings

1 lb. (¾″ thick) boneless
  boneless beef top sirloin steak
1 T. vegetable oil
½ lb. small mushrooms,
  quartered
1 medium onion, sliced
1 clove garlic, minced

1 (12 oz.) jar beef gravy
1 (10 oz.) pkg. frozen
  peas and carrots
¼ tsp. dried thyme
1 (6 oz.) tube refrigerated
  buttermilk biscuits

Preheat oven to 400°. Cut steak in half lengthwise, trimming and discarding any fat. Then cut steak crosswise into ¼″ thick strips. In a large ovenproof skillet over medium high heat, place vegetable oil. Heat beef strips, a few at a time, for 1 to 2 minutes or until outside is no longer pink. Remove from skillet and set aside. In same skillet, combine quartered mushrooms, sliced onions, ¼ cup water and minced garlic. Cook and stir for 3 minutes, or until onions are tender. Stir in gravy, frozen vegetables and thyme. Bring mixture to a boil. Remove from heat and stir in beef strips. Separate refrigerated buttermilk biscuits and cut each biscuit in half. Arrange biscuit halves in a ring over beef mixture in skillet. Bake for 12 to 14 minutes, or until biscuits are golden brown.

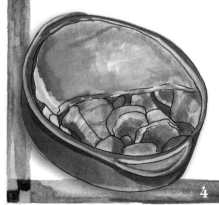

Chicken Alphabet Soup

Makes 6 servings

2 boneless, skinless
  chicken thighs
3 (14 oz. each) cans
  chicken broth

½ C. frozen carrots
1 tsp. yellow mustard
⅔ C. small alphabet
  pasta, uncooked

    Cut chicken thighs into ½″ pieces. Grease a large saucepan with non-stick cooking spray and place over medium high heat. Place chicken pieces in saucepan and heat, stirring occasionally, for 3 minutes. Stir in chicken broth, frozen carrots and yellow mustard, mixing well. Bring mixture to a boil and stir in uncooked alphabet pasta. Return mixture to a boil and cook for 5 to 6 minutes, stirring occasionally, or until carrots and pasta are tender and chicken is thoroughly cooked.

Italian Style Chicken

Makes 4 servings

1 T. vegetable oil
4 boneless chicken
  breast halves
1 (10¾ oz.) can cream
  of mushroom soup

⅓ C. water
1 (14½ oz.) can diced
  tomatoes with
  Italian herbs
1 T. butter or margarine

In a large skillet over medium heat, place vegetable oil, add chicken breast halves and heat, turning once or twice, until browned on all sides. Stir in cream of mushroom soup, water and diced tomatoes with Italian herbs. Bring mixture to a boil. Cover and reduce heat to low. Simmer for 5 minutes, or until chicken is thoroughly cooked. Before serving, stir in butter, mixing until completely melted.

Two-Step Cheesy Pasta

Makes 4 servings

6 C. cooked rotini pasta
1 (26 oz.) jar pasta sauce
1 C. shredded
  mozzarella cheese

½ C. crushed croutons

In a large skillet over medium heat, combine cooked rotini pasta and pasta sauce, tossing until evenly coated and heated throughout. Top with shredded mozzarella cheese and crushed croutons. Cover and heat until cheese is completely melted.

Creamy Chicken & Veggie Pasta

Makes 4 servings

1 T. vegetable oil	1 C. penne pasta,
1 lb. boneless	uncooked
chicken breasts	1 (10¾ oz.) can cream
1 (16 oz.) bag frozen	of chicken soup
mixed vegetables	½ C. water

In a large skillet over medium heat, place vegetable oil. Cut boneless chicken breasts into 1″ pieces. Place chicken in skillet and heat until browned on all sides, stirring often. Add frozen mixed vegetables, penne pasta, cream of chicken soup and water. Bring mixture to a boil. Cover and reduce heat to low. Cook for 10 minutes, or until vegetables are heated and pasta is tender.

Simple Chicken á la King

Makes 4 servings

1 T. vegetable oil	1 (16 oz.) bag frozen
1 lb. boneless	broccoli, cauliflower
chicken breasts	and carrot blend
1 (10¾ oz.) can cream	1 (16 oz.) tube of 8
of chicken soup	buttermilk biscuits

In a large skillet over medium heat, place vegetable oil. Cut boneless chicken breasts into 1″ pieces. Place chicken in skillet and heat until browned on all sides, stirring often. Add cream of chicken soup and frozen vegetable blend to skillet. Cover and let simmer until vegetables are cooked. Meanwhile, prepare buttermilk biscuits according to package directions. Split each biscuit in half and place two split biscuits on each of four plates. Spoon some of the chicken and vegetable mix over biscuits on each plate.

20-Minute Seafood Stew

Makes 4 servings

2 C. prepared pasta sauce
1 (8 oz.) bottle clam juice
¼ C. Burgundy or other
dry red wine
1 (6 oz.) bag frozen
cooked shrimp

½ lb. firm white
fish fillets
1 (6½ oz.) can
chopped clams
Parsley flakes, optional

In a large saucepan over medium heat, combine pasta sauce, clam juice and Burgundy wine. Bring mixture to a boil. Reduce heat to low and let simmer for 5 minutes. Stir in frozen cooked shrimp, white fish pieces and chopped clams. Cover and heat for 5 minutes or until fish and clams are thoroughly heated. Ladle stew into bowls and, if desired, garnish with parsley flakes.

Basil Chicken with Noodles

Makes 4 servings

1 (14 oz.) can chicken broth
½ tsp. dried basil
⅛ tsp. pepper
1 (16 oz.) bag frozen broccoli, cauliflower and carrot blend

2 C. medium egg noodles, uncooked
1 (12½ oz.) can chunk chicken breast, drained

In a large skillet over medium heat, combine chicken broth, dried basil, pepper and frozen vegetable blend. Bring mixture to a boil. Cover and reduce heat to low. Cook for 5 minutes then stir in uncooked egg noodles. Cover and cook for an additional 5 minutes. Add drained chunk chicken and continue to cook, stirring occasionally, until chicken is thoroughly heated.

Five Can Chili

Makes 6 to 8 servings

1 (26 oz.) can
 tomato soup
1 soup can water
2 (11 oz.) cans
 pork n' beans

1 (15 oz.) can kidney
 beans, drained
1 (15½ oz.) can
 chili beans
1 lb. ground beef

In a large soup pot over medium heat, combine tomato soup, water, pork n' beans, drained kidney beans and chili beans. Meanwhile, in a large saucepan over medium high heat, cook ground beef until evenly browned. Drain fat from ground beef and add cooked ground beef to soup pot. Cook, stirring occasionally, 45 minutes or until beans are tender.

Vegetarian Tortilla Pie

Makes 4 to 6 servings

2 (16 oz.) cans
  refried beans
1 (16 oz.) jar
  picante sauce
¼ tsp. garlic powder
2 tsp. dried cilantro
1 (15 oz.) can black beans,
  drained

1 (14½ oz.) can chopped
  tomatoes, drained
7 (8″) flour tortillas
2 C. shredded Cheddar
  cheese

Preheat oven to 400°. In a large mixing bowl, place refried beans. Stir in ¾ cup picante sauce and garlic powder, mixing until well blended. Fold in remaining picante sauce, dried cilantro, drained black beans and drained chopped tomatoes. Place 1 tortilla on a baking sheet. Spread ¾ cup of the pinto bean mixture over the tortilla to within ½″ of the edge. Top with ¼ cup cheese and another tortilla. Spread ⅔ cup black bean mixture over tortilla and top with another ¼ cup cheese. Repeat layers two more times, ending with final tortilla. Spread remaining pinto bean mixture over top tortilla. Cover layered tortillas with aluminum foil and bake for 30 minutes, or until heated throughout. Remove from oven and uncover. Top with remaining shredded cheese and cut into wedges to serve.

Bacon-Wrapped Chicken

Makes 8 servings

8 slices bacon
8 boneless chicken
  breast halves

1 (10¾ oz.) can cream
  of mushroom soup
1 C. sour cream

    Preheat oven to 275°. Wrap 1 bacon slice around each chicken breast half. Place bacon-wrapped chicken in a 7 x 11″ baking dish. In a medium mixing bowl, combine cream of mushroom soup and sour cream. Pour mixture over chicken. Cover baking dish with aluminum foil and place in oven for 2 to 2½ hours, or until chicken is thoroughly cooked.

Chicken Broccoli Bake

Makes 8 servings

1 (16 oz.) bag frozen
chopped broccoli,
thawed and drained
8 boneless chicken
breast halves
1 (26 oz.) can cream
of mushroom soup

⅔ C. milk
¼ tsp. pepper
6 C. prepared instant
white rice

Preheat oven to 400°. Place drained thawed broccoli pieces and chicken breast halves in a large shallow baking dish. In a medium bowl, combine cream of mushroom soup, milk and pepper. Pour mixture over broccoli and chicken in baking dish. Bake for 30 minutes, or until chicken is thoroughly cooked. Divide prepared rice onto 6 to 8 serving plates. Place 1 cooked chicken breast half over rice on each plate and spoon some of the broccoli sauce mixture over each serving.

Quick Hamburger Pizza

Makes two 12" pizzas

½ C. baking and
  pancake mix
1 (¼ oz.) pkg. active
  dry yeast
⅔ C. hot water
1 lb. ground beef
½ C. onion, chopped
1 (15 oz.) can
  tomato sauce

2 tsp. dried oregano
¼ tsp. pepper
½ C. green pepper,
  chopped
2 C. shredded
  mozzarella cheese
1 C. grated
  Parmesan cheese

Preheat oven to 425°. In a large mixing bowl, combine baking mix and active dry yeast. Stir in the hot water and mix until a dough forms. Turn dough onto a floured flat surface and knead 20 times, or until dough is smooth. Set dough aside for about 5 minutes. Meanwhile, in a large skillet over medium heat, combine ground beef and chopped onion. Heat, stirring occasionally, until meat is browned and onions are tender. Drain fat from skillet and stir in tomato sauce, dried oregano and pepper and remove from heat. Divide dough into two parts and roll each part out onto an ungreased 10 x 13" baking sheet or 12" pizza pan, pinching up the edges to form a rim. Spread the meat and vegetable mixture over each dough layer to within ½" of the edge. Sprinkle chopped green pepper, shredded mozzarella cheese and grated Parmesan cheese over meat on each pizza. Bake in oven for 15 to 20 minutes, or until the crust is brown and the filling is hot. Cut into squares or wedges before serving.

Spinach Quiche

Makes 7 servings

1 (10 oz.) pkg. frozen
   chopped spinach,
   thawed and drained
½ onion, chopped
½ C. green pepper,
   chopped
1 C. shredded Cheddar
   cheese

¾ C. baking and
   pancake mix
3 eggs
½ tsp. salt
¼ tsp. pepper

Preheat oven to 400°. Grease the bottom of 9″ pie plate with non-stick cooking spray. Place thawed and drained spinach, chopped onion, chopped green pepper and shredded Cheddar cheese in pie plate. In a large mixing bowl, beat baking mix, eggs, salt and pepper at slow to medium speed until well combined. Pour mixture over other ingredients in pie plate and bake for 35 minutes. For a different look, cut quiche into squares rather than wedges when served.

Simple Hamburger Paprika Pie

Makes 7 servings

1 C. plus 2 tsp. baking
   and pancake mix
⅓ C. heavy
   whipping cream
1 lb. ground beef
2 medium onions

1 tsp. salt
¼ tsp. pepper
2 eggs
1 C. cottage cheese
2 tsp. paprika

Preheat oven to 375°. In a medium bowl, combine 1 cup baking mix and heavy cream, mixing by hand. Knead the dough gently 10 times and press into bottom and up sides of a greased 8″ square baking dish. In a large skillet over medium heat, combine ground beef and onion. Sauté until ground beef is evenly browned and onion is tender. Drain fat. Mix in salt, pepper and additional 2 teaspoons baking mix. Mix well and transfer mixture to baking dish. In a medium mixing bowl, using a wire whisk, beat eggs slightly and blend in cottage cheese. Pour mixture over meat layer in pan. Sprinkle paprika over ingredients and bake for 30 minutes.

Mexican Casserole

Makes 8 to 10 servings

1 lb. ground beef
Salt and pepper to taste
½ C. shredded
   Cheddar cheese
1 C. sour cream
⅔ C. mayonnaise
2 T. chopped onion flakes

2 C. baking and
   pancake mix
½ C. water
2 medium tomatoes,
   thinly sliced
¾ C. chopped
   green pepper

Preheat oven to 375°. In a large skillet over on medium heat, cook ground beef until evenly browned. Drain excess fat from skillet and season with salt and pepper to taste. Remove from heat. In a medium bowl, combine shredded Cheddar cheese, sour cream, mayonnaise and onion flakes, mixing until well combined. In a separate medium bowl, combine baking mix and water, mixing until a soft dough forms. Pat dough out into a greased 9 x 13" baking dish, pressing dough ½" up sides of pan. Place ground beef over dough in baking dish. Layer tomato slices and chopped green pepper over ground beef and top with sour cream mixture. Bake, uncovered, for 25 to 30 minutes, or until the edges of the dough are lightly browned. Remove from oven and let cool for 5 minutes before cutting into squares and serving.

Zucchini Onion Quiche

Makes 10 servings

5 T. butter or margarine,
   melted, divided
½ tsp. dried oregano
¼ tsp. salt
3 small zucchinis, sliced
¼ C. chopped onion

9 eggs
1½ C. milk
½ C. grated
   Parmesan cheese
½ C. baking and
   pancake mix

Preheat oven to 375°. In a large skillet over medium high heat, place 2½ tablespoons melted butter. Add dried oregano, salt, sliced zucchini and chopped onions. Sauté mixture for 5 minutes, or until zucchini and onions are tender. In a blender, combine eggs, milk, cheese, baking mix and remaining melted butter. Process on high until well blended. Pour mixture into a 9 x 13″ baking dish or 12″ pie plate. Spread evenly and top with sautéed zucchini mixture. Bake for 30 to 40 minutes.

Sesame Chicken Wings

Makes about 8 to 10 servings

20 chicken wings
2 eggs
2 T. milk
1½ C. baking and
   pancake mix
½ C. sesame seeds

2 tsp. paprika
1½ tsp. dry mustard
½ tsp. salt
¼ C. butter or
   margarine, melted

Preheat oven to 425°. Lightly grease two 9 x 13″ baking dishes and set aside. Separate chicken wings at joints, discarding the tips. In a medium bowl, whisk together eggs and milk. In a separate mixing bowl, combine baking mix, sesame seeds, paprika, dry mustard and salt. Dip chicken pieces first into the egg mixture and then in the sesame seed mixture, tossing until evenly coated. Place chicken wings in prepared baking dishes and drizzle melted butter over chicken in both dishes. Bake, uncovered, for 35 to 40 minutes, or until chicken is browned and crispy.

Sweet & Sour Chicken

Makes 4 servings

¼ C. baking and
   pancake mix
¼ C. crushed cornflakes
¼ tsp. salt
¼ tsp. paprika
⅛ tsp. pepper
4 boneless chicken
   breast halves

1 (9 oz.) jar sweet
   and sour sauce
1 small green pepper,
   cut into ¼″ strips
1 (8½ oz.) can pineapple
   chunks, drained

In a large ziplock bag, place baking mix, crushed cornflakes, salt, paprika and pepper. Moisten chicken breast halves with cold water. Place chicken in bag, one piece at a time, and shake until evenly coated. Repeat with remaining chicken pieces. Arrange chicken in an 8″ square glass baking dish. Cover baking dish with waxed paper and place in microwave. Heat on high for 8 minutes. Rotate dish and return to microwave for an additional 6 to 8 minutes, or until chicken is thoroughly cooked. In a large glass measuring cup, place sweet and sour sauce, green pepper strips and drained pineapple chunks. Cover measuring cup with waxed paper and heat in microwave for 3 minutes. Remove from microwave and stir. Recover and heat in microwave for an additional 2 to 3 minutes, or until green pepper is tender but crisp. Place cooked chicken pieces on a serving platter and drizzle sauce over chicken.

Swiss Cheese & Sausage Deep Dish Pie

Makes 4 servings

1 (8 oz.) pkg. frozen
  cooked breakfast
  sausages
1 C. baking and
  pancake mix
¼ C. cold water

1 (6 oz.) pkg. shredded
  Swiss cheese
2 eggs
¼ C. milk
¼ tsp. salt
⅛ tsp. pepper

Preheat oven to 375°. Thaw and heat sausages according to package directions and drain fat from sausage. Grease a 9″ round pie plate and set aside. In medium bowl, combine baking mix and water, mixing until a soft dough forms. Press dough into bottom and 1″ up sides of pie plate. Arrange cooked sausages over dough with points facing in, so sausages appear like the spokes of a wheel. Sprinkle shredded Swiss cheese over sausages. In medium bowl, whisk together eggs, milk, salt and pepper. Mix well and pour over sausages and cheese in pie plate. Bake for 25 minutes, or until crust is puffed and golden brown.

Wagon Wheel Hash Brown Casserole

Makes 6 servings

1 (8 oz.) pkg. frozen
   cooked breakfast
   sausages
3 C. frozen hash browns
½ C. chopped green
   onions
½ tsp. salt
1 (8 oz.) pkg. cream
   cheese, softened

⅓ C. plus 2 T. milk,
   divided
¼ tsp. pepper
¾ C. baking and
   pancake mix
2 eggs

Preheat oven to 400°. Grease a 10″ pie plate and set aside. In a large skillet over medium heat, heat sausages until thoroughly cooked. Drain fat from skillet and set sausages aside. Spread thawed hash browns in an even layer across bottom of pie plate. In medium bowl, combine chopped green onions, salt, softened cream cheese, ⅓ cup milk and pepper. Mix until well combined and spread mixture over potatoes in pie plate. Arrange cooked sausages over cream cheese mixture with points facing in, like the spokes of a wheel. In a medium bowl, combine baking mix, remaining 2 tablespoons milk and eggs, whisking until well blended. Pour mixture around sausages in pie plate and bake, uncovered, for 25 to 30 minutes, or until crust is puffed and golden brown.

Beef & Tomato Casserole

Makes 8 to 10 servings

3 C. cooked beef tips
1 C. chopped onion
1 C. thinly sliced celery
2 (15 oz.) cans chopped
   tomatoes, drained
1½ C. shredded Swiss
   cheese

2¼ C. milk
¼ C. butter, melted
5 eggs
1¼ C. baking and
   pancake mix
½ tsp. garlic salt

Preheat oven to 350°. Grease a 9 x 13″ baking dish. Layer cooked beef tips, chopped onion, sliced celery, chopped tomatoes and shredded Swiss cheese in baking dish. In a large mixing bowl, beat milk, melted butter, eggs, baking mix and garlic salt at high speed for 1 minute, or until smooth. Pour mixture over ingredients in baking dish. Bake for 40 to 45 minutes, or until a knife inserted in center of dish comes out clean. Remove from oven and let cool for 5 minutes before serving.

Beer Battered Shrimp

Makes 10 servings

1¼ C. baking and
   pancake mix, divided
3 (6 oz.) bags frozen
   cooked shrimp

½ tsp. salt
1 egg
½ C. beer

In a shallow dish, place ¼ cup baking mix. Roll shrimp until lightly coated in baking mix. In a medium mixing bowl, combine remaining 1 cup baking mix, salt, egg and beer, whisking together until smooth. Dip shrimp into beer batter, allowing excess batter to drip back into the bowl. Fill a large skillet with 2″ vegetable oil and place over medium high heat until oil registers 350° on a kitchen thermometer. Add small batches of coated shrimp to hot oil and fry for 1 to 2 minutes. Carefully remove shrimp with a slotted spoon and set on paper towels to drain. Repeat with remaining coated shrimp until all is cooked.

Breaded Pork Chops

Makes 8 servings

½ C. baking and pancake mix	¼ tsp. pepper
12 saltine crackers, crushed	1 egg
	2 T. water
1 tsp. seasoned salt	8 (½″ thick) boneless pork loin chops

In a medium bowl, combine baking mix, crushed saltine crackers, seasoned salt and pepper. In a second bowl, combine egg and water, whisking until smooth. Dip pork chops first into egg mixture and then into the baking mix, turning to coat on both sides. Grease a large non-stick skillet with cooking spray and place over medium high heat. Place pork chops in skillet and heat for 8 to 10 minutes, turning once, until pork is cooked and only slightly pink in the center.

Burrito Bake

Makes 7 servings

1 lb. ground beef
1 (16 oz.) can refried
  beans
1 C. baking and
  pancake mix

¼ C. water
1 C. salsa
1½ C. shredded
  Cheddar cheese
3 green onions, chopped

Preheat oven to 375°. Grease a 9″ pie pan with non-stick cooking spray and set aside. In large skillet over medium heat, cook ground beef until evenly browned. Drain fat from skillet and set ground beef aside. In a medium bowl, combine refried beans, baking mix and water, mixing until well combined. Spread mixture in pie pan and press into bottom and sides of pan. Spoon browned ground beef into pie pan and top with salsa, shredded Cheddar cheese and chopped green onions. Bake for 30 minutes.

Ham & Cauliflower Au Gratin

Makes 8 servings

1 (16 oz.) bag frozen
  cauliflower
1 (10 oz.) pkg. deli sliced
  smoked ham
1 (11 oz.) can Cheddar
  cheese soup
¼ C. milk

⅔ C. baking and
  pancake mix
2 T. butter or margarine
2 T. shredded
  Cheddar cheese
½ tsp. ground nutmeg

Preheat oven to 400°. Arrange frozen cauliflower in an even layer across bottom of a 7 x 11″ baking dish. Chop deli sliced ham into pieces and sprinkle over cauliflower. In a medium bowl, beat Cheddar cheese soup and milk with a whisk until smooth. Pour mixture over ham. In a medium bowl, combine baking mix, butter, shredded Cheddar cheese and ground nutmeg, mixing until crumbly. Sprinkle mixture over ingredients in baking dish. Bake for 20 to 25 minutes, or until topping is golden brown.

Stuffed Chicken Squares

Makes 6 servings

1 (3 oz.) pkg. cream
   cheese, softened
3 T. mayonnaise
1 (12½ oz.) can chunk
   chicken breast, drained
1 C. shredded
   Cheddar cheese
¼ C. thinly sliced celery
¼ C. chopped green
   onions
½ (4 oz.) jar
   diced pimentos

½ tsp. garlic salt
⅛ tsp. pepper
2 C. baking and
   pancake mix
½ C. cold water
2 T. butter or
   margarine, melted
½ C. finely crushed
   corn chips

Preheat oven to 400°. In a large bowl, combine softened cream cheese, mayonnaise, drained chicken, Cheddar cheese, celery, onions, diced pimentos, garlic salt and pepper. In a medium bowl, mix baking mix and water, stirring vigorously until a soft dough forms. Gently smooth dough into a ball and knead 5 times. Roll dough into a 12 x 18″ rectangle and cut into 6 even squares. Spoon about ⅓ cup of the chicken mixture onto center of each square. Bring 4 corners of dough to center of chicken mixture and twist together at the top, pressing edges together to seal chicken mixture inside. Brush melted butter over tops of chicken squares. Dip filled squares into corn chips until lightly coated and place on an ungreased cookie sheet. Bake for 20 minutes, or until golden brown.

Roast Beef, Corn & Tomato Bake

Makes 4 to 6 servings

3 (8 oz.) tubs deli sliced
  cooked roast beef
1 (16 oz.) can corn,
  drained
1 (14½ oz.) can
  tomato soup
1 C. shredded
  Cheddar cheese

1 T. dry onion flakes
1 tsp. chili powder
1 (12 oz.) tube refrigerated
  buttermilk biscuits
2 T. butter or
  margarine, melted
¼ C. corn meal

    Preheat oven to 400°. Chop deli sliced roast beef into smaller pieces. In a medium bowl, combine chopped roast beef, drained corn, tomato soup, Cheddar cheese, dry onion flakes and chili powder. Mix until well combined and transfer mixture to a 9 x 13″ baking dish. Bake for 10 minutes. Meanwhile, separate buttermilk biscuits and roll each biscuit in corn meal until evenly coated. Arrange biscuits on top of ingredients in baking dish and return to oven for an additional 20 to 25 minutes.

Baked Corned Beef Sandwiches

Makes 8 servings

2 C. baking and
  pancake mix
½ C. cold water
1 (15 oz.) can corned
  beef hash
Mustard

Mayonnaise
2 (2¼ oz.) cans
  sliced olives
1 (8 oz.) pkg. sliced
  Swiss cheese
1 small onion, sliced

Preheat oven to 425°. In a medium mixing bowl, combine baking mix and water, stirring to form a dough. Roll out dough on a floured surface and shape into a ¼″ thick 8 x 12″ rectangle. Transfer dough to an ungreased baking sheet. Spread corned beef hash over dough layer and top with a layer of mustard and mayonnaise. Top with sliced olives, Swiss cheese slices and onion slices. Bake for 12 to 20 minutes, or until crust is golden brown. Remove from oven and cut in squares before serving.

Bacon Swiss Dinner Pie

Makes 8 servings

1 (3 oz.) box fully cooked
   bacon, crumbled
1 C. shredded
   Swiss cheese
⅓ C. chopped onion

2 C. milk
4 eggs
1 C. baking and
   pancake mix
⅛ tsp. pepper

Preheat oven to 400°. Grease a 10″ pie plate and spread crumbled bacon, shredded Swiss cheese and chopped onion in an even layer across bottom of pie plate. In blender, place milk, eggs, baking mix and pepper. Process on high for 15 seconds, or until well blended. Pour mixture over ingredients in pie plate. Bake for 35 to 40 minutes, or until a toothpick inserted in center of dish comes out clean. Remove from oven and let cool 5 minutes before serving.

Asparagus Parmesan Brunch Pie

Makes 6 servings

1 (15 oz.) can asparagus
  spears, drained
1 C. sour cream
1 C. cottage cheese
½ C. baking and
  pancake mix

2 eggs
1 (15 oz.) can chopped
  tomatoes, drained
¼ C. grated
  Parmesan cheese

Preheat oven to 350°. Grease a 9″ pie plate. Spread drained asparagus spears in an even layer across bottom of pie plate. In blender, process sour cream, cottage cheese, baking mix, melted butter and eggs at high speed for 15 seconds, or until smooth. Pour mixture over asparagus in pie plate and top with chopped tomatoes. Sprinkle grated Parmesan cheese over all and bake for 30 minutes, or until toothpick inserted in center of dish comes out clean. Remove from oven and let cool 5 minutes before serving.

Excellent Pepperoni Pizza Bake

Makes 6 servings

1 medium onion,
  chopped
⅓ C. grated
  Parmesan cheese
½ C. baking and
  pancake mix
1 C. milk
2 eggs

1 (8 oz.) can pizza sauce
½ (3½ oz.) pkg. sliced
  pepperoni
¼ C. chopped
  green pepper
¾ C. shredded
  mozzarella cheese

Preheat oven to 400°. Grease 9″ pie pan and sprinkle chopped onion and grated Parmesan cheese evenly across bottom of pan. In medium bowl, combine baking mix, milk and eggs, mixing until blended. Pour mixture into pie pan and bake for 20 minutes. Remove from oven and spread pizza sauce over baked layer. Top with sliced pepperoni, chopped green pepper and shredded mozzarella cheese. Return to oven for an additional 10 to 15 minutes, or until cheese is lightly browned. Remove from oven and let cool for 5 minutes before serving.

Vegetable Beef Casserole with Biscuits

Makes 8 servings

1 lb. ground beef,
  cooked and drained
1 (15 oz.) can corn,
  drained
1 (14½ oz.) can
  sliced peas and
  carrots, drained

1 (10¾ oz.) can
  tomato soup
1 T. Italian seasoning
½ tsp. chili powder
1 (6 oz.) tube refrigerated
  buttermilk biscuits

Preheat oven to 350°. In a medium mixing bowl, combine browned ground beef, drained corn, drained carrots, tomato soup, Italian seasoning and chili powder. Mix until well combined and transfer mixture to a 9 x 13″ baking dish. Cover baking dish with aluminum foil and bake for 25 minutes. Meanwhile, separate dough into individual biscuits. After 25 minutes, place biscuits over ingredients in baking dish and return to oven for an additional 10 minutes, or until biscuits are browned and thoroughly cooked.

Oven-Baked Maple Pancake

Makes 12 servings

1½ C. baking and
pancake mix
1 T. sugar
2 eggs
¾ C. milk

1½ C. shredded Swiss
cheese, divided
¼ C. maple syrup
1 (3 oz.) box fully cooked
bacon, crumbled

Preheat oven to 425°. Grease and flour a 9 x 13″ baking dish and set aside. In medium bowl, beat baking mix, sugar, eggs, milk, ½ cup shredded Swiss cheese and maple syrup with an electric mixer at medium speed until smooth. Pour mixture into prepared dish. Bake, uncovered, for 10 to 15 minutes, or until a toothpick inserted in center of dish comes out clean. Remove from oven and sprinkle remaining shredded Swiss cheese and crumbled bacon over top. Return to oven and bake for an additional 3 to 5 minutes, or until cheese is melted. If desired, serve with additional maple syrup.

Oven Fried Chicken

Makes 4 servings

1 T. butter or margarine	1¼ tsp. salt
⅔ C. baking and	¼ tsp. pepper
pancake mix	4 boneless skinless
1½ tsp. paprika	chicken breasts

Preheat oven to 425°. Place butter in a 9 x 13″ baking dish and place baking dish in oven until butter has melted. In a medium bowl, combine baking mix, paprika, salt and pepper, stirring until well combined. Place chicken pieces in dry mixture and turn until completely coated. Place coated chicken pieces in prepared baking dish. Bake, uncovered, for 35 minutes. Turn chicken pieces over and return to oven for an additional 15 minutes, or until chicken is thoroughly cooked.

Reuben Casserole with Rye Biscuits

Makes 12 servings

1 (27 oz.) can sauerkraut, rinsed and drained
1 (14½ oz.) can diced tomatoes, drained
¼ C. Thousand Island dressing
¼ C. plus 2 T. butter, softened, divided
2 (3 oz.) pkgs. sliced corned beef
2 C. shredded Swiss cheese

2⅔ C. baking and pancake mix
¼ C. crushed rye crackers
1 tsp. cocoa powder
2 tsp. molasses
½ tsp. caraway seeds
⅔ C. milk
½ C. mayonnaise
½ C. yellow mustard
1 tsp. dry onion flakes

Preheat oven to 425°. In an ungreased 9 x 13″ baking dish, spread sauerkraut in an even layer. Arrange drained diced tomatoes over sauerkraut and spread Thousand Island dressing over tomatoes. Place 2 tablespoons butter dotted over dressing layer. Top with corned beef and shredded Swiss cheese. Bake for 15 minutes. Meanwhile, in a medium bowl, combine baking mix, rye cracker crumbs, remaining ¼ cup softened butter, cocoa powder, molasses and caraway seeds, mixing until well blended. Add milk and, using a fork, stir mixture into a dough. Smooth dough into ball and knead 10 times on a lightly floured flat surface. Roll dough out to ½″ thickness and cut into circles using a biscuit cutter. Arrange biscuits evenly over ingredients in baking dish and return to oven for an additional 15 to 20 minutes. Meanwhile, in a small bowl, combine mayonnaise, mustard and dry onion flakes, mixing until smooth. Serve casserole with mustard sauce on the side.

Cheesy Biscuit Tuna Casserole

Makes 8 servings

⅓ C. chopped
  green peppers
⅓ C. chopped onion
3 T. butter or margarine
2¼ C. baking and
  pancake mix, divided
1 (10¾ oz.) can cream
  of mushroom soup
¾ C. milk

1 (6½ oz.) can tuna,
  drained
1 T. lemon juice
1 (16 oz.) can peas and
  carrots, drained
½ C. cold water
¾ C. to 1 C. shredded
  American cheese

Preheat oven to 425°. In a medium saucepan over medium heat, place chopped green peppers, chopped onion and butter. Sauté until vegetables are softened. Stir in ¼ cup baking mix and add cream of mushroom soup, mixing until well combined. Gradually stir in milk. Bring mixture to a boil for 1 minute, stirring constantly. Stir in drained tuna, lemon juice and drained peas and carrots. Mix well and transfer to a 7 x 11″ baking dish. Place baking dish in oven to keep hot while preparing biscuits. In medium mixing bowl, combine remaining 2 cups baking mix and cold water, mixing until a soft dough forms. Shape dough into a ball and knead 5 times on a lightly floured flat surface. Roll dough out into a 9 x 15″ rectangle. Sprinkle shredded American cheese over dough and roll dough up tightly, beginning at wide side. Seal dough by pinching edges. Cut rolled up dough into twelve 1¼″ slices. Remove dish from oven and place biscuits, cut side down, over tuna mixture. Return to oven and bake for 20 to 25, or until biscuits are browned and cooked throughout.

Parmesan Zucchini Pie

Makes 8 servings

1 (10¾ oz.) can
  French onion soup
4 C. grated zucchini
½ C. grated
  Parmesan cheese
2 T. dried parsley flakes

1 C. baking and
  pancake mix
½ tsp. nutmeg
¼ tsp. salt
¼ tsp. pepper
2 eggs, beaten

Preheat oven to 350°. Grease a 9 x 13″ baking dish with non-stick cooking spray and set aside. In a medium bowl, combine French onion soup, grated zucchini, grated Parmesan cheese, dried parsley flakes, baking mix, nutmeg, salt, and pepper, mix well. Stir in beaten eggs and oil. Pour mixture into prepared pan and bake for 25 minutes. Cut into triangles or squares and serve.

Slow Cooker Chicken n' Dressing Casserole

Makes 6 servings

1 (24 oz.) loaf whole grain wheat bread, cubed
1¼ C. chicken broth
1 (10¾ oz.) can cream of mushroom soup
¼ C. butter or margarine, melted
¼ C. olive oil
1 C. chopped celery
1 C. chopped onion
1 tsp. chicken bouillon granules
1 tsp. dried sage
½ tsp. pepper
4 skinless boneless chicken breast halves, cooked and diced

Preheat oven to 375°. Spread bread cubes in a single layer on two baking sheets. Bake for 10 minutes, or until bread cubes are lightly toasted. In a medium bowl, combine chicken broth, cream of mushroom soup, melted butter and olive oil. Mix chopped celery, chopped onion, chicken bouillon granules, dried sage, and pepper into chicken broth mixture. Place toasted bread cubes in a medium bowl and pour chicken broth mixture over bread cubes, tossing until bread cubes are completely coated. In a slow cooker, spread ½ of the bread cube mixture in an even layer. Spread half of the cooked diced chicken over bread cubes. Top with another layer of the bread cube mixture and remaining cooked diced chicken. Cover and cook on low setting for 4 to 6 hours.

Easy Beef Stroganoff

Makes 6 servings

4 C. wide egg noodles, uncooked
1 lb. (¼″ thick) beef round tip steaks
4 tsp. vegetable oil, divided
1 clove garlic, minced
¼ tsp. salt
¼ tsp. pepper
1 (8 oz.) pkg. sliced mushrooms
1 (¾ oz.) pkg. brown gravy mix
1 C. cold water
¼ C. sour cream

Prepare egg noodles according to package directions. Cut round tip steaks in half lengthwise and then cut crosswise into 1″ wide thick strips. In a large non-stick skillet over medium high, place 2 teaspoons vegetable oil. Place beef strips and minced garlic in skillet and stir-fry for 1 to 2 minutes, or until outside surface of beef is no longer pink. Remove meat from skillet and season beef strips with salt and pepper. Place remaining 2 teaspoons vegetable oil in the same skillet over medium high heat. Add sliced mushrooms to skillet and heat, stirring occasionally, for 2 minutes or until mushrooms are tender. Remove mushrooms from skillet. Place gravy mix and cold water in skillet and mix well. Bring gravy mixture to a boil, reduce heat and let simmer for 1 minute, or until sauce is thickened, stirring frequently. Stir in cooked beef strips, cooked mushrooms and sour cream, tossing until heated throughout. Serve over prepared egg noodles.

Pork & Veggie Skillet

Makes 4 servings

2 T. butter or margarine
4 boneless pork loin
  chops, diced
1 (12 oz.) jar pork gravy
2 T. ketchup

2 (15 oz.) can sliced
  white potatoes, drained
1 (16 oz.) pkg. frozen
  mixed vegetables

In a large skillet over medium high heat, place butter and diced pork loin. Heat, stirring frequently, for 3 to 5 minutes, or until pork pieces are evenly browned. Stir in pork gravy, ketchup and drained sliced potatoes. Cover and let simmer 10 minutes. Stir in frozen mixed vegetables and cook for an additional 10 to 15 minutes, or until vegetables are tender and pork is thoroughly cooked.

Quick n' Easy Chili Pie

Makes 6 to 8 servings

1½ lbs. ground beef
1 (1 oz.) pkg. onion
   soup mix
1 (15 oz.) can red kidney
   beans or black beans,
   drained
1½ C. water

1 (8 oz.) can
   tomato sauce
1 T. chili powder
1 T. hot pepper sauce
1 (10 oz.) bag corn chips
1 (8 oz.) pkg. shredded
   Cheddar cheese

In a large skillet over medium high heat, brown ground beef and drain fat. Stir in onion soup mix, drained beans, water, tomato sauce, chili powder and hot pepper sauce. Bring mixture to a boil, reduce heat, cover and let simmer for 20 minutes, stirring occasionally. Arrange corn chips evenly in a 9 x 13″ baking dish and spoon hot chili over top. Sprinkle shredded Cheddar cheese over all and serve immediately.

Crispy Rice Meatloaf

1½ lbs. ground beef
⅓ lb. ground pork
   sausage
1 (10¾ oz.) can tomato
   soup, divided

1 C. crispy rice cereal
¼ C. evaporated milk
1 C. diced onions
1 T. ground sage
½ tsp. salt

Preheat oven to 350°. In a large mixing bowl, combine ground beef and sausage. Mix in ½ can of tomato soup, crispy rice cereal, evaporated milk, diced onions, ground sage and salt. Mix until well combined and transfer mixture to a 5 x 9″ loaf pan. Pour remaining tomato soup over loaf. Place aluminum foil loosely over loaf pan like a tent. Bake for 1½ hours, or until meat loaf is cooked throughout.

Beef Tenderloin in Red Wine Sauce

Makes 4 to 6 servings

1 (1 oz.) pkg. onion soup mix	1 (750 ml.) bottle red wine 1 (2 lb.) beef tenderloin

In a large saucepan over medium heat, combine onion soup mix and red wine, stirring constantly until soup mix is completely dissolved. Place beef tenderloin in a large ziplock bag. Pour half of wine mixture into bag with beef tenderloin. Place remaining half of the wine mix in a container and chill in refrigerator. Place ziplock bag with beef tenderloin in refrigerator and marinate for 2 hours. Preheat oven to 400°. Remove beef from bag, discard marinade and place tenderloin in a large skillet. Sear beef over medium high heat, turning to brown all sides. Remove beef from frying pan and place in a large roasting pan. Pour reserved wine mixture over tenderloin and bake for 50 minutes for a medium rare doneness. Remove from oven and place beef on a serving platter. Pour pan drippings into a medium saucepan over medium high heat. Heat mixture, stirring occasionally, until sauce has reduced to desired thickness.

Stir Fry Pork in Sherry Sauce

Makes 4 servings

1 lb. boneless pork
  tenderloin
1 (8 oz.) pkg. frozen
  baby whole sweet
  corn, thawed
½ C. water
2 T. soy sauce
2 T. dry cooking sherry
4 tsp. cornstarch
½ tsp. chicken bouillon
  granules

1 T. vegetable oil
2 cloves garlic, minced
3 medium carrots,
  thinly sliced
1 (4 oz.) pkg. sliced
  shitake or other
  fresh mushrooms
1 (6 oz.) pkg. frozen
  pea pods, thawed
3 C. hot cooked rice

Trim fat from pork tenderloin and place pork in freezer until partially frozen. Remove from freezer and slice across the grain into thin strips. Cut baby corn in half crosswise. In a medium bowl, combine water, soy sauce, dry cooking sherry, cornstarch and chicken bouillon granules and set aside. In a large skillet over medium high heat, place vegetable oil. Add minced garlic and sauté for 15 seconds. Add thinly sliced carrots and heat, tossing occasionally, for 3 minutes. Mix in sliced mushrooms and sliced baby corn. Stir fry for an additional 1 to 2 minutes, or until vegetables are crisp but tender. Remove the vegetables from the skillet and set aside. Add half of the pork slices to skillet and stir fry for 2 to 3 minutes, or until no longer pink. Remove pork from skillet and repeat with remaining pork slices. Return all pork to the skillet and add sauce mixture to center of the skillet. Cook and stir until sauce is thickened and bubbly. Return cooked vegetables to skillet and mix in pea pods. Stir fry mixture until heated throughout and evenly coated in sauce. Serve immediately with hot cooked rice.

Slow Cooker Stuffed Peppers

Makes 6 servings

6 green sweet
  bell peppers
½ medium onion
1 lb. lean ground beef
1 pkg. chicken flavored
  rice mix
1 (15 oz.) can corn,
  drained

1½ tsp. Worcestershire
  sauce
1 tsp. salt
¼ tsp. pepper
1 C. shredded
  mozzarella cheese
1 (8 oz.) can
  tomato sauce

Wash green peppers and cut ½″ off the top of each pepper. Scoop out seeds from peppers and discard. Chop the tops of the peppers and onion in small pieces and set aside. In a large skillet over medium heat, sauté ground beef until browned and drain fat from skillet. Return beef to skillet and add chopped onions and peppers and sauté until softened. In a medium bowl, combine cooked ground beef mixture, rice mix, drained corn, Worcestershire sauce, salt, pepper and shredded mozzarella cheese. Mix until well combined and scoop mixture evenly into the six peppers. Lightly coat the inside of a slow cooker with non-stick cooking spray and place filled peppers in slow cooker. Pour the tomato sauce evenly over the peppers. Cover and cook on low setting for 6 to 8 hours or on high setting for 3 to 4 hours.

Porcupine Meatballs

Makes 30 meatballs

1½ C. crispy rice cereal
squares, crushed
1 lb. ground beef
⅔ C. long-grain
converted rice,
uncooked
½ C. milk

1 (1 oz.) pkg. onion
soup mix
1 egg
1 C. water
2 (11½ oz.) cans
tomato juice

Preheat oven to 425°. In a large bowl, combine crushed rice cereal squares, ground beef, uncooked converted rice, milk, onion soup mix and egg. Mix until well combined and shape mixture into 30 meatballs. Place meatballs in an ungreased 9 x 13″ baking dish. Pour water and tomato juice over meatballs and stir gently. Cover baking dish and place in oven. Bake for 50 to 55 minutes, or until rice is tender and meatballs are no longer pink in center.

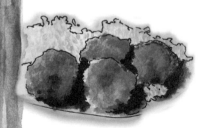

Baseball
Taco Caps

Makes 12 servings

2 C. crispy rice cereal
squares, crushed
2 C. flour
1 (1¼ oz.) pkg. taco
seasoning mix, divided
¼ tsp. baking powder
¼ tsp. garlic powder
½ C. butter or margarine

½ C. warm water
½ lb. ground beef
¾ C. shredded
Cheddar cheese
1 (14 oz.) can diced
tomato, drained
¾ C. shredded lettuce

Preheat oven to 375°. In large bowl, combine crushed cereal squares, flour, half of the taco seasoning mix, baking powder and garlic powder, tossing until well combined. Using a pastry blender, cut in butter until coarse crumbs form. Gradually stir in warm water, mixing until a soft dough forms. If dough is too dry, add more water, 1 tablespoon at a time. Divide dough into 2 parts and cover with a damp towel until ready to use. On a lightly floured flat surface, roll out each part dough to ¹⁄₁₆″ thickness. Cut each piece into six 4″ circles. Place one dough circle in each of 6 cups of a two separate 12-cup muffin pans, alternating cups, making sure dough is even with rim of muffin cup on one side of each. On opposite side of each, extend dough over rim and press down firmly to form the "bill" of each cap. Press dough evenly onto bottom and up sides of muffin cups. Bake for 15 to 20 minutes, or until golden brown. Remove from oven and carefully remove caps from muffin cups and let cool. To prepare filling, in a medium skillet over medium high heat, combine ground beef and remaining taco seasoning mix, heating until ground beef is evenly browned. Drain fat from skillet and fill each baked "cap" with equal amounts of seasoned ground beef, shredded cheese, diced tomato and shredded lettuce.

Tuna Macaroni Casserole

Makes 4 to 6 servings

1 (7 oz.) pkg. elbow
    macaroni, uncooked
1 C. milk
½ tsp. salt
¼ tsp. pepper
1 (10¾ oz.) can cream
    of mushroom soup
1 (10 oz.) pkg. frozen
    mixed vegetables,
    thawed

1 (6 oz.) can tuna
    in water, drained
2 C. crispy rice cereal
    squares, crushed
1 T. butter or
    margarine, melted
½ C. shredded
    Cheddar cheese

Preheat oven to 400°. Prepare macaroni according to package directions and drain. In an ungreased 2-quart casserole dish, combine milk, salt, pepper, cream of mushroom soup, mixed vegetables, drained tuna and prepared macaroni. In a small bowl, using a fork, toss together crushed rice cereal squares and melted butter. Sprinkle cereal mixture over ingredients in casserole dish. Bake, uncovered, for 30 minutes, or until casserole is bubbly around the edges and heated through. Remove from oven and sprinkle with shredded Cheddar cheese. Let sit for 5 minutes before serving.

Breaded Chicken Nuggets

Makes about 25 pieces

3 C. crispy rice cereal
squares, crushed
½ C. grated
Parmesan cheese
½ tsp. salt
½ tsp. seasoned salt
¼ tsp. paprika

⅛ tsp. garlic powder
3 T. butter or
margarine, melted
1 T. milk
1 lb. boneless skinless
chicken breasts

Preheat oven to 400°. Line a baking sheet with aluminum foil and set aside. In medium bowl, combine crushed rice cereal squares, grated Parmesan cheese, salt, seasoned salt, paprika and garlic powder, tossing until well combined. In a small bowl, combine melted butter and milk. Cut chicken breasts into 1″ pieces. Dip chicken pieces first into butter mixture and then into cereal mixture, tossing until evenly coated. Arrange coated chicken pieces on prepared baking sheet. Bake for 9 minutes. Turn chicken pieces over and bake for an additional 8 minutes, or until coating is light golden brown and chicken is thoroughly cooked. Remove nuggets from oven and serve with sweet and sour sauce, ranch dressing or barbecue sauce.

Delicious Crunchy Breakfast Bake

Makes 12 servings

1 (6 oz.) pkg. deli sliced cooked ham, chopped
1 medium green pepper, chopped
2 T. dry onion flakes
1 (4 oz.) can mushroom pieces, drained
5 C. crispy rice cereal squares

1 C. shredded Cheddar cheese
1 C. baking and pancake mix
2 C. milk
4 eggs

Preheat oven to 375°. Grease a 9 x 13″ baking dish and set aside. In a 10″ non-stick skillet, heat chopped ham, chopped green pepper, dry onion flakes and drained mushroom pieces. Cook for 3 minutes, stirring frequently, until heated throughout. Spread 3 cups of the rice cereal squares evenly across bottom of prepared baking dish. Sprinkle ham mixture over cereal layer and top with shredded Cheddar cheese. In a large glass measuring cup, combine baking mix, milk and eggs, whisking until well combined. Pour mixture evenly over shredded cheese and sprinkle remaining cereal over all. Bake, uncovered, for and 25 to 30 minutes or until a toothpick inserted in center of dish comes out clean.

Chex-Mex Casserole

Makes 8 servings

4½ C. crispy rice cereal squares, divided
1 (15 oz.) can red kidney beans in water

1½ C. salsa
2 C. shredded Cheddar cheese, divided
Sour cream, optional

Preheat oven to 350°. In an 8″ square baking dish, spread 2½ cups rice cereal squares in an even layer. Spoon red kidney beans over cereal layer and sprinkle 1 cup shredded Cheddar cheese over beans. Spoon salsa evenly over cheese layer and top with remaining cereal squares. Sprinkle remaining shredded Cheddar cheese over top. Bake, uncovered, for 20 to 25 minutes, or until mixture is heated throughout and cheese is melted. Remove from oven and, if desired, serve hot with sour cream.

Deep Dish Crispy Chicken Pie

Makes 8 servings

3 (12½ oz.) cans chunk chicken breast, drained
½ C. milk
1½ tsp. dry onion flakes
1 (10 oz.) pkg. frozen mixed vegetables, thawed
1 (10¾ oz.) can cream of chicken soup
1 (4 oz.) can mushroom pieces, drained
4 C. crispy rice cereal squares
3 T. butter or margarine, melted
⅓ C. grated Parmesan cheese

Preheat oven to 350°. In a large bowl, combine drained chunk chicken, milk, dry onion flakes, mixed vegetables, cream of chicken soup and drained mushroom pieces. Spread mixture evenly into an ungreased 9 x 13″ baking dish. In medium mixing bowl, toss together rice cereal squares and melted butter, mixing until cereal is evenly coated. Stir in grated Parmesan cheese and spoon mixture over chicken mixture in baking dish. Bake, uncovered, for 35 minutes.

Philly Ranch Cheese Steaks

Makes 4 servings

1 C. thinly sliced onions
1 C. thinly sliced green
  peppers
3 T. olive oil
1 lb. beef sirloin steak,
  sliced into ¼″ thick
  strips

½ C. prepared Cheddar
  and Parmesan dressing
4 hoagie sandwich rolls
½ C. shredded
  mozzarella cheese

In a large skillet over medium high heat, sauté sliced onions and sliced peppers in olive oil for 5 minutes, or until softened. Add steak strips and sauté for an additional 5 to 7 minutes, or until meat is thoroughly cooked. Remove from heat and mix in dressing. Pile ¼ of the meat mixture onto each hoagie sandwich roll. Top meat on each sandwich with shredded mozzarella cheese. If desired, spread an additional 1 teaspoon dressing on each roll. Preheat broiler. Place sandwiches open faced on broiler pan and place under broiler for 1 minute, or until cheese is melted and bread is toasted.

Mediterranean Turkey Bake

Makes 4 servings

1 C. sliced mushrooms
½ C. diced red onion
½ C. diced red
  bell pepper
1 T. olive oil
2 C. hot cooked rice
¼ C. diced green chilies

2 T. dried parsley flakes
2 (7 oz.) pkgs. deli sliced
  cooked turkey, chopped
¾ C. Cheddar and
  Parmesan dressing
½ C. shredded Swiss
  cheese

Preheat oven to 350°. In a large skillet over medium heat, sauté mushrooms, diced onion and diced pepper in olive oil until soft. Stir in cooked rice, diced green chilies and dried parsley flakes, tossing until softened and heated throughout. Transfer mixture to an 8″ square baking dish. In a small bowl, toss together chopped turkey and dressing. Spoon turkey mixture over mixture in baking dish. Sprinkle shredded Swiss cheese over turkey mixture. Bake for 20 minutes, or until cheese is completely melted.

Pasta & Chicken in Creamy White Wine Sauce

Makes 8 servings

1 (12 oz.) pkg. fettuccine or egg noodles, uncooked
1 C. creamy Italian dressing
⅓ C. Dijon mustard

8 boneless skinless chicken breast halves, pounded thin
½ C. butter or margarine
⅓ C. dry white wine

Preheat oven to 425°. Cook pasta according to package directions and drain. In a small bowl, combine creamy Italian dressing and Dijon mustard. Pour cooked pasta in a lightly greased 9 x 13″ baking dish. In a large skillet over medium high heat, sauté chicken breasts in butter, turning once to heat both sides. Place cooked chicken breasts over cooked pasta. Add dry white wine to skillet and cook to reduce to desired thickness. Drizzle wine sauce over chicken and pour remaining dressing mixture and mustard mixture over chicken. Bake for 10 minutes, or until dressing forms a golden brown crust and chicken is thoroughly cooked.

Turkey Rice Casserole with Bagel Chips

Makes 4 servings

¾ lb. ground turkey
1 (6½ oz.) pkg. broccoli
  au gratin rice mix
2½ T. butter or
  margarine

2¼ C. water
2 C. frozen mixed
  vegetables, thawed
1 (6 oz.) bag bagel chips
  any kind

In a large skillet over medium high heat, brown ground turkey until evenly cooked. Drain fat from skillet and set cooked ground turkey aside. In same skillet over medium heat, sauté pasta from rice mix in butter until pasta is light golden brown. Slowly stir in water and seasoning packet from rice mix. Bring mixture to a boil, reduce heat to low, cover and let simmer for 10 minutes. Stir in mixed vegetables and cooked ground turkey. Cover and let simmer for 5 to 7 minutes or until rice is tender. Let stand 3 to 5 minutes before serving. Serve with bagel chips on the side.

Baked Chicken n' Rice Rolls

Makes 8 servings

1 (6½ oz.) pkg. chicken
and mushroom rice mix
8 boneless skinless
chicken breast halves
¼ C. milk
½ C. crushed butter
flavor crackers

¼ C. butter or
margarine, melted
¼ tsp. dried thyme
⅛ tsp. pepper

Preheat oven to 375°. In a large skillet, prepare rice mix according to package directions. Set aside and let cool for 10 minutes. Pound each chicken breast half to ¼″ thickness. Spoon ⅓ cup of the prepared rice mixture over each chicken breast half. Roll up chicken breast halves enclosing rice mixture and secure with wooden toothpicks. Dip rolled chicken in milk and roll in crushed crackers. Arrange rolled chicken in a 9 x 13″ baking dish and set aside. In a small bowl, combine melted butter, dried thyme and pepper. Drizzle butter mixture evenly over chicken. Bake for 40 to 45 minutes, or until chicken is thoroughly cooked. Remove wooden toothpicks before serving.

Seasoned Turkey Meatballs

Makes 20 meatballs

1 (6¾ oz.) pkg. any flavor rice mix
1 lb. ground turkey

1 egg, beaten
1 T. vegetable oil
2½ C. water

In large mixing bowl, combine pasta from rice mix, ground turkey and beaten egg. Shape mixture into twenty 1″ to 2″ meatballs. In a large skillet over medium high heat, brown meatballs in vegetable oil and drain. Slowly stir in water and seasoning packet from rice mix. Bring mixture to a boil. Cover and reduce heat to low and let simmer for 30 minutes, or until meatballs are thoroughly cooked.

Chicken Teriyaki Bowls

Makes 4 servings

1 (6¼ oz.) pkg. chicken
   teriyaki rice mix
2 T. butter or margarine
2⅓ C. water
2 C. frozen mixed
   vegetables
1 lb. boneless skinless
   chicken breasts,
   cut into thin strips

½ C. chopped
   red pepper
¼ C. teriyaki sauce
Chopped nuts or chow
   mein noodles

In a large skillet over medium heat, sauté pasta from rice mix in butter until pasta is golden brown. Add water and seasoning packet from rice mix to skillet. Increase heat to high and bring mixture to a boil. Cover, reduce heat to low and let simmer for 10 minutes. Stir in frozen mixed vegetables, cover and let simmer for an additional 10 to 13 minutes or until rice and vegetables are tender. Meanwhile, in a separate skillet over medium heat, sauté chicken and chopped red bell pepper for 4 to 5 minutes, or until chicken is thoroughly cooked. Stir in teriyaki sauce. Remove skillet from heat, cover and let stand. To serve, divide rice mixture evenly into four bowls and top rice in each bowl with an even amount of the Teriyaki chicken mixture. If desired, garnish with chopped nuts or chow mein noodles.

Noodle Beef Skillet

Makes 4 servings

1 lb. ground beef
2 C. medium egg
 noodles, uncooked
1 (15 oz.) can corn,
 drained

6 green onions, sliced
1 C. water
½ C. salsa
2 (8 oz.) cans
 tomato sauce

In a large skillet over medium high heat, brown ground beef until evenly cooked. Drain fat from skillet and stir in uncooked egg noodles, drained corn, sliced green onions, water, salsa and tomato sauce. Mix well and bring mixture to a boil. Reduce heat to low, cover and let simmer. Cook, stirring occasionally, for 10 to 12 minutes or until noodles are cooked to desired doneness. Serve with bread rolls.

Fiesta Dinner with Cheddar Baked Biscuits

Makes 5 servings

1 lb. ground beef
½ C. chopped onion
¾ C. salsa
1 (11 oz.) can Mexican corn with red and green peppers, drained
1 (8 oz.) can tomato sauce
1 tsp. sugar
½ tsp. plus ⅛ tsp. garlic powder, divided

½ tsp. chili powder
⅛ tsp. pepper
2 T. cornmeal
½ tsp. paprika
1 (12 oz.) tube refrigerated biscuits
1 T. butter or margarine, melted
1 C. shredded Cheddar cheese

Preheat oven to 375°. In a large oven-safe skillet over medium heat, brown ground beef and sauté chopped onion until thoroughly cooked. Drain fat from skillet and stir in salsa, drained Mexican corn, tomato sauce, sugar, ½ teaspoon garlic powder, chili powder and pepper. Bring mixture to a boil, reduce heat to low and let simmer for 10 to 15 minutes, or until most of liquid is absorbed. Meanwhile, in a small bowl, combine cornmeal, paprika and remaining ⅛ teaspoon garlic powder, mixing until well combined. Separate refrigerated dough into 10 biscuits and cut each biscuit in half crosswise. Arrange biscuits, cut side down, around outer edge of hot beef mixture in skillet. Brush melted butter over biscuits and sprinkle cornmeal mixture over top. Sprinkle shredded Cheddar cheese in center of skillet over beef mixture. Bake for 15 to 20 minutes, or until biscuits are golden brown.

Roasted Pork with Seasoned Vegetables & Stuffing

Makes 6 servings

2 medium sweet potatoes,
  peeled and cubed
1 red onion, cut into
  thin wedges
½ C. Catalina dressing
1½ tsp. dried thyme,
  divided

1 (6 oz.) pkg. chicken
  stuffing mix
1½ C. water
2 (¾ lb. each) pork
  tenderloins

Preheat oven to 375°. Grease an 11 x 15″ jellyroll pan and set aside. In a medium bowl, toss cubed sweet potatoes and onion wedges with dressing and ½ teaspoon dried thyme. Arrange coated sweet potatoes and onions in a single layer on the prepared pan. Bake for 10 minutes. Meanwhile, in a medium mixing bowl, combine stuffing mix and water. Cut each tenderloin diagonally into thirds. Push vegetable mixture to edges of pan and spoon stuffing mixture down center of pan. Top with tenderloin pieces. Sprinkle remaining 1 teaspoon dried thyme over pork. Bake for 45 to 50 minutes, or until pork is thoroughly cooked.

Pork Chop French Onion Skillet

Makes 6 servings

1 tsp. vegetable oil
6 boneless pork chops,
  cut ½˝ thick
2 medium onions,
  thinly sliced
2 T. Worcestershire sauce

1 (6 oz.) pkg. chicken
  stuffing mix
1½ C. hot water
1 C. shredded Swiss
  cheese

In a large skillet over medium high heat, place vegetable oil. Add pork chops and thinly sliced onions and cook for 10 minutes, or until chops are cooked through, tossing onions occasionally and turning chops after 5 minutes. Transfer cooked pork chops to a plate and cover to keep warm. Sauté onions for an additional 5 minutes, or until golden brown. Add Worcestershire sauce and mix well. Reduce heat to low and return chops to skillet. Spoon onion mixture evenly over chops. In medium bowl, combine stuffing mix and hot water. Spoon stuffing mixture around edge of skillet and sprinkle with shredded Swiss cheese. Cover and cook for an additional 5 minutes, or until stuffing is heated through and cheese is melted.

Classic Stuffing Meatloaf

Makes 6 servings

1½ lb. ground beef
1 (10¾ oz.) can tomato
  soup, divided
1 (6 oz.) pkg. chicken
  stuffing mix

1 egg, lightly beaten
1 onion, chopped
1 tsp. dried thyme
¼ C. chili sauce

Preheat oven to 350°. Grease a 5 x 9″ loaf pan with non-stick cooking spray and set aside. In a large bowl, combine ground beef, ½ cup tomato soup, stuffing mix, beaten egg, chopped onion and dried thyme, mixing by hand until well combined. Press mixture evenly into prepared loaf pan. Bake for 55 minutes. In a small saucepan over low heat, combine remaining tomato soup and chili sauce, mixing until well combined. Remove meatloaf from oven and spoon chili sauce mixture over top. Serve with boiled quartered potatoes, carrots and celery, if desired.

Slow Cooked BBQ Short Ribs

Makes 4 servings

4 lbs. beef short ribs
1 large onion,
   coarsely chopped
1 C. barbecue sauce

¼ C. honey
¼ C. flour
1 T. prepared mustard

Place ribs and chopped onions in slow cooker. In medium bowl, combine barbecue sauce, honey, flour and mustard, mixing until well combined. Pour mixture over ribs and onions in slow cooker and cover with lid. Cook on low setting for 6 to 8 hours, or until ribs are tender. Remove ribs from slow cooker and cover to keep warm. Skim excess fat from sauce and return ribs to sauce. Stir gently until ribs are evenly coated.

Chili Mac & Cheeseburger Skillet

Makes 4 servings

1 lb. ground beef
2 C. water
1 (7¼ oz.) pkg. macaroni
and cheese dinner
1 tsp. chili powder

1 (16 oz.) pkg. frozen
chopped broccoli,
thawed
¼ C. ketchup

In a large skillet over medium heat, cook ground beef until evenly browned and drain fat from skillet. Stir in water, macaroni noodles and chili powder. Bring mixture to boil and cover. Reduce heat to low heat and let simmer for 5 minutes, stirring occasionally. Add thawed broccoli and simmer for an additional 5 minutes, or until noodles are tender. Stir in cheese sauce mix and ketchup, mixing until blended.

Corn Dog Stuffing

Makes 4 servings

1⅔ C. water   **5 hot dogs, sliced**
¼ C. butter or margarine
1 (6 oz.) pkg. cornbread
   stuffing mix

In a medium saucepan over medium high heat, combine water and butter. Bring to a boil and stir in cornbread stuffing mix. Add sliced hot dogs and mix until well incorporated. Reduce heat, cover and let simmer for 5 minutes.

Ham, Cheese & Vegetable Skillet

Makes 6 servings

2 C. water
2 C. elbow macaroni, uncooked
1 (8 oz.) block processed cheese food, cut into pieces
2 (6 oz.) pkgs. thin sliced smoked ham, chopped
2 C. frozen mixed vegetables, thawed

In a large skillet over high heat, bring water to a boil. Stir in macaroni, reduce heat to medium low, cover, and let simmer for 8 to 10 minutes, or until macaroni is tender. Add processed cheese pieces, chopped ham and mixed vegetables. Heat, stirring frequently, until cheese is completely melted.

Grilled Pork Chops with Seasoned Rice

Makes 4 servings

6 T. Italian dressing
2 T. apricot jam
  or preserves
4 bone-in or boneless
  pork chops
1½ C. instant white rice,
  uncooked

2 C. green beans,
  trimmed
1 (14½ oz.) can
  chicken broth

Preheat grill to medium high heat. In a medium bowl, combine Italian dressing and apricot jam, mixing with a wire whisk until well blended. Brush some of the dressing mixture over pork chops and let stand for 10 minutes. Meanwhile, place rice in the center of a 12″ square sheet of heavyduty aluminum foil. Place trimmed green beans over rice and drizzle 2 tablespoons dressing mixture over all. Bring up sides of aluminum foil, forming a bowl. Gradually pour chicken broth and remaining 2 tablespoons dressing mixture over beans. Fold top ends of foil together to form a sealed packet, leaving a little room for heat circulation inside. Place chops and foil packet on grate of preheated grill. Grill packet 15 minutes, or until most of the liquid has been absorbed. Let stand 5 minutes. Grill pork chops, turning once, for 20 minutes, or until thoroughly cooked.

Steak Salad with Italian Avocado Dressing

Makes 4 servings

2 beef top round steaks
Chili powder to taste
8 C. mixed salad greens
1 C. halved cherry
   tomatoes

¼ C. red onion slices
⅓ C. Italian dressing
½ medium ripe avocado,
   peeled and pitted
½ C. mixed nuts

Preheat grill to medium high heat. Sprinkle desired amount of chili powder over steaks. Place steaks on grill for 5 to 7 minutes. Turn steaks over and grill for an additional 5 to 7 minutes, or until cooked through. Remove steak from grill and cover loosely with aluminum foil. Let stand 5 minutes. Cut steak across the grain into thin slices. Place steak strips in a clear glass serving bowl. Layer salad green, halved tomatoes and red onion slices over steak. In a blender, place Italian dressing and peeled avocado. Cover and process on high until well blended. Drizzle mixture over salad ingredients and top with mixed nuts.

Tomato Beef & Pasta Bake

Makes 4 servings

**1 (14 oz.) pkg. macaroni
and cheese dinner
1 lb. ground beef**

**1 (15 oz.) can chopped
tomatoes, drained
2 T. dried parsley flakes**

Prepare macaroni and cheese dinner according to package directions. In a large skillet over medium high heat, cook ground beef until evenly browned. Drain fat from skillet and mix in prepared macaroni and cheese, chopped tomatoes and dried parsley flakes. Toss until well mixed and serve.

One Pan Roast Pork & Apple Dinner

Makes 4 servings

4 (¾″ thick) pork chops
1 onion, sliced
3 (4 oz.) cans mushroom
  pieces, drained
2 T. balsamic
  vinaigrette dressing
1½ C. instant white rice,
  uncooked

1 (10½ oz.) can
  chicken broth
1 (10½ oz.) can water
2 red apples, sliced
1 tsp. dried thyme

Grease a large non-stick skillet with cooking spray. Place pork chops in skillet and cook for 4 minutes on each side, or until evenly browned. Add sliced onion, drained mushroom pieces and vinaigrette to skillet. Heat for an additional 3 minutes and stir in instant rice, chicken broth, water, sliced apples and dried thyme. Reduce heat to medium and let simmer for 10 minutes, or until mixture is heated throughout.

April Fool's Dinner Pie

Makes 6 servings

1 lb. ground beef
½ C. thick 'n chunky
   salsa
1 (15 oz.) can corn,
   drained
1 (10 oz.) pkg.
   shredded carrots
¼ C. dry bread crumbs

2 (15 oz.) cans whole
   white potatoes, drained
   and cut into quarters
½ (16 oz.) pkg. frozen
   cauliflower florets,
   thawed
¼ C. milk
¼ tsp. salt

Preheat oven to 400°. In a large bowl, combine ground beef, salsa, drained corn, shredded carrots and dry bread crumbs, mixing until well blended. Mix well and press mixture evenly into a 9″ pie plate. Bake for 30 minutes, or until meat is no longer pink. Meanwhile, in a large saucepan over medium high heat, place quartered potatoes and thawed cauliflower florets. Add enough water to completely cover vegetables and bring mixture to a boil. Reduce heat to medium low and let simmer for 20 minutes, or until vegetables are tender. Drain liquid from vegetables and stir in milk and salt. Using an electric mixer, mash vegetables until light and fluffy. Spread mashed mixture over meat mixture and serve.

Shipwreck
Dinner Skillet

Makes 4 servings

1 lb. ground beef
1 (7¼ oz.) pkg. macaroni
  and cheese dinner
1 (16 oz.) can stewed
  tomatoes in juice

1 C. frozen peas
1 C. milk
1 C. shredded
  mozzarella cheese

In a large non-stick skillet on medium high heat, cook ground beef until evenly browned. Drain fat from skillet and stir in macaroni, cheese sauce mix, stewed tomatoes, frozen peas and milk. Bring mixture to boil, reduce heat to medium low, cover, and let simmer for 12 minutes, or until macaroni is tender. Sprinkle shredded mozzarella cheese over all. Remove from heat and let stand for 5 minutes until cheese is melted.

Herbed Crusted Pork Chops with Cheesy Macaroni

Makes 8 servings

8 boneless pork chops	1 (24 oz.) pkg. shells
1 tsp. Italian seasoning	and cheese dinner
1 T. vegetable oil	2 (10 oz. each) pkg.
3 C. water	frozen green beans

Sprinkle both sides of pork chops with Italian seasoning. In a large soup pot over medium heat, heat vegetable oil. Place pork chops in a skillet, two at a time, cooking for 4 to 5 minutes on each side, or until thoroughly cooked. Remove chops to plate and cover to keep warm while cooking remaining chops. Add water to oil in soup pot and bring to boil. Stir in shell pasta. Reduce heat to medium low, cover, and let simmer for 10 minutes. Add frozen green beans and cover. Continue to cook for 6 minutes, or until pasta is tender and beans are heated through. Drain liquid from pot and stir in cheese sauce, mixing until evenly coated. Serve pork chops with macaroni mixture on the side.

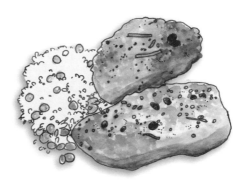

Slow Cooker Hawaiian Pork

Makes 8 servings

2 lbs. boneless pork
  loin, sliced
½ C. honey
  barbecue sauce
1 (20 oz.) can pineapple
  chunks in juice
3 T. cornstarch

2 large green peppers,
  coarsely chopped
2 large red peppers,
  coarsely chopped
6 C. hot cooked instant
  white rice
¼ C. chopped peanuts

Place pork loin slices in slow cooker. Add barbecue sauce, mixing until pork is evenly coated. Drain pineapple, reserving ¼ cup of the juice. In a medium bowl, combined reserved pineapple juice and cornstarch, stirring until well blended. Pour cornstarch mixture over pork in slow cooker, stirring until well blended. Place pineapple chunks, chopped green peppers and chopped red peppers over pork in slow cooker. Cover and cook on high setting for 5 hours, or until pork is tender and thoroughly cooked. Place pork slices over hot cooked rice on a serving platter and sprinkle with chopped peanuts.

One Pot Italian Pasta

Makes 8 servings

2 lb. ground beef
2 cloves garlic, minced
1 (14½ oz.) can diced
   tomatoes in juice
1 (14½ oz.) can
   beef broth
1 C. water
2 C. bowtie pasta,
   uncooked

1 medium zucchini,
   sliced
1 (6 oz.) can tomato paste
¼ tsp. Italian seasoning
1 C. shredded Cheddar
   cheese

In a large skillet over medium heat, combine ground beef and minced garlic. Heat until ground beef is evenly browned and drain fat from skillet. Return ground beef to skillet and add tomatoes in juice, beef broth and water. Mix well and bring mixture to a boil. Stir in uncooked bowtie pasta and sliced zucchini. Cover, reduce heat to medium and let simmer for 15 minutes, or until pasta is tender. Stir in tomato paste and Italian seasoning, mixing until well blended. Sprinkle shredded Cheddar cheese over all and stir lightly until cheese is melted.

Tangy Grilled Pork Steaks

Makes 6 servings

½ C. spicy steak sauce
¼ C. Dijon mustard
2 tsp. crushed red
   pepper flakes

6 (4 oz.) pork steaks,
   cut ¾″ thick

Preheat grill to medium high heat. In a medium bowl, combine spicy steak sauce, Dijon mustard and crushed red pepper flakes. Place pork steaks in a large ziplock plastic bag. Add steak sauce mixture to plastic bag, seal bag tightly and turn steaks to coat both sides. Let marinate in refrigerator for 1 hour, turning bag over occasionally. Remove steaks from bag and discard marinade. Place steaks on grill and heat for 5 to 7 minutes on each side, or until thoroughly cooked.

Papaya Grilled Pork Tacos

Makes 8 servings

1 C. barbecue sauce
2 C. peeled and chopped
   papaya, divided
½ C. Dijon mustard
2 T. ground cumin
1¼ lbs. boneless
   country style pork ribs

1 T. dried crushed
   mint leaves
2 tsp. pepper
12 flour tortillas,
   warmed

Preheat grill to medium high heat. In a blender, combine barbecue sauce, 1 cup chopped papaya, Dijon mustard and ground cumin. Cover and process until smooth. Pour mixture into a large ziplock plastic bag. Place pork ribs in bag and seal. Place in refrigerator and let marinade for 4 hours, turning bag occasionally. Remove ribs from bag and discard marinade. Place ribs on grill and heat for 12 to 15 minutes on each side, or until thoroughly cooked. Remove ribs from grill and use 2 forks to shred the meat from the bone. In a medium bowl, combine remaining 1 cup papaya, dried crushed mint and pepper. Spoon 1 tablespoon of the papaya mixture and ¼ cup of the shredded pork over each tortilla. Roll up tortillas and serve.

Cheddar Macaroni Lasagna

Makes 4 servings

1 (14 oz.) pkg. macaroni
  and cheese dinner
1 lb. ground beef
1 (14 oz.) jar spaghetti
  sauce

½ C. shredded
  mozzarella cheese

Preheat oven to 375°. Prepare macaroni and cheese according to package directions. In a large skillet over medium heat, cook ground beef until evenly browned and drain fat from skillet. Stir in spaghetti sauce and mix well. In an 8″ square baking dish, spread half of meat mixture. Top with half of macaroni dinner. Repeat layers with remaining ground meat and remaining macaroni and cheese. Sprinkle shredded mozzarella cheese over top. Bake for 15 minutes, or until heated throughout.

Steak & Scalloped Potato Skillet

Makes 5 servings

1 lb. boneless beef sirloin
  steak, cut into strips
1 medium onion, sliced
1 T. vegetable oil

1 (10½ oz.) pkg. cheesy
  scalloped potato mix
½ C. milk
2½ C. hot water

    In a large skillet over medium high heat, sauté steak strips and sliced onion in vegetable oil until steak is thoroughly cooked. Stir in potatoes from scalloped potato mix, milk and hot water. Bring mixture to boil, reduce heat to medium low and cover. Let simmer, stirring occasionally, for 12 to 15 minutes, or until potatoes are tender. Stir in cheese sauce packet from potato mix, tossing until well blended.

Cheesy Shepherd's Pie

Makes 4 servings

½ (11¾ oz.) pkg.
  cheesy mashed
  potato mix
1 lb. ground beef

1 C. frozen mixed
  vegetables
1 C. beef gravy

Preheat oven to 375°. Prepare cheesy mashed potatoes according to package directions. In a large skillet over medium heat, cook ground beef until evenly browned and drain fat from skillet. Stir in mixed vegetables and beef gravy, mixing until well combined. Spoon meat mixture into a casserole dish. Top meat with prepared mashed potatoes. Bake in oven for 20 to 25 minutes, or until potatoes are lightly browned.

Country Seasoned Chops

Makes 6 servings

1 (16 oz.) bag frozen
   potato wedges
1 (16 oz.) bag
   baby carrots
1 C. onion wedges
¾ C. Italian dressing

6 (6 oz.) boneless pork
   chops, cut ½″ thick
1 env. pork
   seasoning mix
¼ C. grated Parmesan
   cheese

Preheat oven to 400°. In a 9 x 13″ baking dish, place frozen potato wedges, baby carrots and onion wedges Drizzle Italian dressing over vegetables, tossing until evenly coated. Coat pork chops with pork seasoning mix according to package directions. Discard any remaining seasoning mix. Place seasoned pork chops over vegetables in baking dish. Bake for 45 minutes, or until chops are thoroughly cooked and vegetables are tender. Remove from oven and sprinkle with grated Parmesan cheese over all.

Cabbage Skillet Dinner

Makes 4 servings

¾ lb. ground beef
1 medium yellow onion, chopped
1 (¾ oz.) env. Italian salad dressing mix
1 (28 oz.) can crushed tomatoes

2 (16 oz.) bags Cole slaw mix
1 C. water
1 C. brown rice, uncooked

In a large skillet over medium high heat, combine ground beef, chopped onion and Italian salad dressing mix. Heat for 4 to 6 minutes, or until meat is evenly browned. Stir in crushed tomatoes and Cole slaw mix. Heat, stirring occasionally, until Cole slaw mix is slightly softened. Reduce heat, cover and let simmer for 20 to 25 minutes, or until cabbage is tender. Stir in water and brown rice and bring mixture to a boil. Cover, reduce heat and cook for 25 minutes. Remove from heat, stir and cover. Let stand for 5 minutes before serving.

Barbecued Stir-Fry

Makes 4 servings

½ C. peppercorn
 ranch dressing
½ tsp. curry powder
1 lb. boneless beef sirloin
 steak, cut into thin slices

1 (12 oz.) pkg. frozen
 stir-fry vegetables
2 C. instant white rice,
 uncooked

Preheat grill to medium high heat. In a medium bowl, combine peppercorn ranch dressing and curry powder. Place a large saucepan over grate of grill. Add 2 tablespoons of the dressing mixture and thin steak slices to skillet. Cook and stir-fry for 5 minutes or until steak is evenly browned. Add remaining dressing mixture and frozen stir-fry vegetables to skillet. Cook and stir for 5 to 10 minutes, or until vegetables are crisp but tender and steak is cooked throughout. Cook instant rice according to package directions. Divide rice evenly onto four plates and top rice on each plate with a generous amount of the steak and vegetable stir-fr.

Quick Jambalaya

Makes 6 servings

1 T. vegetable oil
½ lb. hot Italian sausage,
   sliced and quartered
1 medium onion, chopped
1 (14 oz.) can diced
   tomatoes in juice
1 (14½ oz.) can
   chicken broth

1 medium green pepper,
   chopped
½ C. barbecue sauce
1 lb. frozen cooked
   shrimp, thawed
2 C. instant white rice,
   uncooked

In a large non-stick skillet over medium high heat, heat vegetable oil. Stir in quartered sausage and chopped onion, heating until sausage is no longer pink. Add diced tomatoes in juice, chicken broth, chopped green pepper, barbecue sauce, thawed shrimp and uncooked rice, mixing until well combined. Bring to a boil and cover. Remove from heat and let stand for 5 minutes. Stir gently before serving.

Cheesy Ham & Cauliflower Bake

Makes 8 servings

2 lbs. ground
  smoked ham
1 (4 oz.) sleeve saltine
  crackers, crushed
1 small onion, chopped
1 T. prepared horseradish

½ C. milk
2 eggs, lightly beaten
1 C. Cheez Whiz
2 (16 oz.) bags frozen
  cauliflower florets,
  cooked

Preheat oven to 350°. In a large bowl, combine ground ham, saltine cracker crumbs, chopped onion, horseradish, milk and beaten eggs, mixing until well blended. Press ham mixture evenly into an ungreased 10″ ring mold. Bake for 45 minutes, or until heated throughout. Remove from oven and turn ham mold out onto a serving platter. Heat cheese dip according to package directions. Fill center of ham ring with the cooked cauliflower and drizzle hot cheese dip over all. Serve immediately.

Beef & Noodle Spinach Stew

Makes 6 servings

1 (5½ oz.) pkg. small
   shell pasta
1 (14½ oz.) can
   beef broth
1 (14½ oz.) can diced
   tomatoes in juice
2 T. steak sauce

¼ tsp. crushed
   red pepper flakes
2 (6 oz.) bags
   spinach leaves
¾ lb. boneless beef
   round steak, cut into
   thin strips

Cook pasta according to package directions and drain. In a large saucepan over medium high heat, combine beef broth, tomatoes in juice, steak sauce and crushed red pepper flakes. Bring mixture to a boil for 3 minutes. Stir in cooked pasta and spinach leaves. Return mixture to boil. Reduce to medium low heat and let simmer for 2 minutes. Stir in steak strips and cook for 2 to 3 minutes, or until steak strips are thoroughly cooked.

Roast in Mushroom Sauce

Makes 8 servings

½ C. steak sauce
1 (4½ oz.) jar sliced
  mushrooms in water
⅛ tsp. garlic powder
1 (2 lb.) beef eye
  round roast

1 T. cornstarch
¼ C. cold water
1 (8 oz.) pkg. egg
  noodles, cooked

Preheat oven to 350°. In a medium bowl, combine steak sauce, mushrooms with liquid and garlic powder, mixing until well blended. Place roast in 9 x 13″ baking dish and pour steak sauce mixture over roast. Cover baking dish tightly with aluminum foil. Bake for 2 hours. Remove roast from pan and place on a heated platter and cover to keep warm. Pour mushroom mixture from pan into a medium saucepan. In a separate bowl, combine cornstarch and water, mixing until cornstarch is completely dissolved. Add cornstarch mixture to saucepan. Cook over medium high heat, stirring frequently, until mixture thickens and begins to boil. Remove saucepan from heat and cover to keep warm. Cut roast into thin slices and serve with the mushroom sauce and prepared egg noodles.

Peach & Dijon Glazed Ham

Makes 20 servings

½ C. orange marmalade
1 (8 oz.) can sliced
   peaches, drained
   and chopped
⅓ C. Dijon mustard

2 T. cooking sherry
1 (4 lb.) fully cooked
   boneless ham
¼ C. water

Preheat oven to 325°. In a medium mixing bowl, combine orange marmalade, chopped peaches, Dijon mustard and cooking sherry. Mix until well combined and set aside. Remove wrapping from ham and place ham in a shallow baking dish. Add water to pan and cover tightly with aluminum foil. Bake for 1½ hours. Remove aluminum foil and spoon ½ cup marmalade mixture over entire surface of ham. Return to oven and bake for an additional 30 minutes, or until heated through. Heat remaining marmalade mixture in a small saucepan over low heat and serve with sliced ham.

Teriyaki Steak with Brown Rice

Makes 4 servings

1 T. vegetable oil
1 lb. boneless beef sirloin
   steak, cut into strips
1½ C. water
⅓ C. teriyaki sauce
½ tsp. garlic powder

2 C. brown rice,
   uncooked
1 (12 oz.) pkg. frozen
   broccoli florets
½ C. chopped peanuts
   or cashews, optional

Heat vegetable oil in a non-stick skillet over medium high heat. Add steak strips to skillet and cook, stirring lightly, until steak is evenly browned. Add water, teriyaki sauce and garlic powder, stirring constantly. Bring mixture to boil and stir in brown rice, broccoli florets and, if desired, chopped peanuts. Cook over low heat for 25 minutes. Remove from heat and let stand 5 minutes before serving.

Taco Skillet Fiesta

Makes 6 servings

1 lb. ground beef
1 small onion, chopped
1 (1¼ oz.) pkg. taco
  seasoning mix
2 C. corn chips

½ lb. (8 oz.) block
  processed cheese
  food, cut into pieces
1 (14½ oz.) can diced
  tomatoes, drained

In a large skillet over medium high heat, sauté ground beef and chopped onion until meat is evenly browned and onions are softened. Drain fat from skillet and stir in taco seasoning mix. Sprinkle corn chips over meat mixture and top with cheese pieces. Cover and cook over low heat for 5 minutes, or until cheese is completely melted. Sprinkle chopped tomatoes over cheese and serve immediately.

Cornbread Sloppy Joes

Makes 4 servings

1 (8½ oz.) pkg.
   corn muffin mix
1 lb. ground beef
¾ C. barbecue sauce
½ C. shredded
   Cheddar cheese

1 (14½ oz.) can chopped
   tomatoes, drained
½ C. chopped
   green pepper

Preheat oven to 400°. Prepare corn muffin batter according to package directions and bake in an 8″ or 9″ round baking dish for 20 to 25 minutes, or until a toothpick inserted in center of dish comes out clean. Remove from oven and let cool slightly. In a large skillet over medium heat, brown meat and drain off fat. Stir in barbecue sauce. Reduce heat to low and let simmer for 10 to 15 minutes, or until heated throughout, stirring occasionally. Cut cornbread into 4 wedges and place 1 wedge on each serving plate. Spoon ½ cup of the meat mixture over each cornbread wedge. Top each serving with some of the shredded Cheddar cheese, drained tomatoes and chopped green peppers.

Cheesy Pizza Mac

Makes 6 servings

1 lb. ground beef
2 C. water
1 (15 oz.) can pizza sauce
2 C. elbow macaroni,
　uncooked

1½ C. Italian style
　shredded cheese,
　divided
12 slices pepperoni

In a large skillet over medium heat, cook ground beef until evenly browned and drain fat from skillet. Stir in water and pizza sauce. Bring mixture to boil and mix in uncooked macaroni. Reduce heat to medium low, cover and let simmer for 8 to 10 minutes, or until macaroni is tender. Stir in half of the shredded cheese. Sprinkle remaining shredded cheese and pepperoni slices over top. Remove skillet from heat and let stand, covered, for 2 minutes, or until cheese is completely melted.

Glazed Pork Chops with Peach Stuffing

Makes 6 servings

1 (8½ oz.) can peach
 slices in juice
Hot water
1 (6 oz.) pkg. pork
 stuffing mix
¼ C. butter or margarine,
 cut into pieces

6 (½″ thick) pork chops
⅓ C. peach or apricot
 preserves
1 T. Dijon mustard

Preheat oven to 375°. Drain peaches, reserving 1 cup of the syrup. In a large bowl, place reserved 1 cup peach syrup and add enough hot water to measure 1½ cups. Add seasoning packet from stuffing mix and butter, mixing until butter is completely melted. Stir in crumbs from stuffing mix and drained peaches. Set aside and let stand for 5 minutes. Spoon stuffing mixture into a 9 x 13″ baking dish. Arrange pork chops over stuffing mixture in baking dish. In a small bowl, combine apricot preserves and Dijon mustard. Spoon mixture over pork chops and bake for 40 minutes, or until chops are thoroughly cooked.

Pot Roast, Veggies & Gravy

Makes 8 servings

1 (2½ lb.) beef pot roast, trimmed of fat
2 tsp. vegetable oil
1½ C. water, divided
¾ C. brewed coffee
Pepper
1 (16 oz.) bag baby carrots

2 C. frozen potato wedges
1 (15 oz.) can diced tomatoes, drained
1 onion, sliced
2 T. flour
4 C. cooked brown rice

In a non-stick Dutch oven over medium high heat, place vegetable oil. Brown meat on all sides and add 1 cup water and brewed coffee. Season with pepper to taste and bring mixture to a boil. Reduce heat, cover and let simmer for 1 hour. Add baby carrots, potato wedges, drained diced tomatoes and onion slices to Dutch oven. Cover and let simmer for an additional 45 minutes, or until roast is cooked through and vegetables are tender. Place meat and vegetables on a serving platter, reserving liquid in Dutch oven. Keep meat warm. In a medium bowl, combine remaining ½ cup water and flour, mixing until well blended. Gradually add flour mixture to hot liquid in Dutch oven. Cook until mixture boils and thickens, stirring constantly. Simmer for 3 minutes, stirring constantly. Slice roast across the grain into thin slices and serve with vegetables, sauce mixture and prepared brown rice.

Tropical Frank n' Beans

Makes 10 servings

½ C. chopped
  green pepper
1 T. butter or margarine
1 (16 oz.) pkg. hot dogs,
  sliced

1 (16 oz.) can
  pork n' beans
1 (20 oz.) can pineapple
  chunks, drained
½ C. barbecue sauce

In a large saucepan over medium heat, sauté chopped green peppers in butter until softened. Add sliced hot dogs, pork n' beans, drained pineapple chunks and barbecue sauce. Cook until ingredients are thoroughly heated, stirring occasionally.

Teriyaki Beef Stir-Fry

Makes 4 servings

1 T. vegetable oil
1 lb. beef sirloin steak,
  cut into strips
1 (12 oz.) pkg. frozen
  stir-fry vegetables

¾ C. teriyaki sauce
2 C. cooked instant
  white rice

In a large skillet over medium high heat, heat vegetable oil. Add steak strips to skillet and cook for 5 minutes, stirring often, until steak is thoroughly cooked. Add frozen stir-fry vegetables and teriyaki sauce, mixing well. Cover and cook for 3 to 4 minutes, or until vegetables are crisp but tender, stirring frequently. Serve over hot cooked rice.

15 Minute Spinach Pie

Makes 6 servings

3 eggs
¾ C. milk
2 C. chicken stuffing mix
1 (10 oz.) pkg. frozen
  chopped spinach,
  thawed
12 slices thin smoked
  ham, chopped

¾ C. cottage cheese
⅓ C. green onion slices
¼ tsp. garlic powder
⅓ C. shredded
  Cheddar cheese

In a large bowl, beat eggs and milk with wire whisk until well blended. Add stuffing mix, thawed spinach, chopped ham, cottage cheese, green onion slices and garlic powder, mixing until well combined. Spoon mixture into a greased 9″ glass pie plate. Cover pie plate loosely with waxed paper. Microwave on high for 5 minutes. Remove from microwave and stir gently to completely mix the center with the outside edge. Smooth top and replace waxed paper. Microwave for an additional 5 minutes, or until center is no longer wet. Remove from microwave and sprinkle with shredded Cheddar cheese, let stand, covered, for 5 minutes or until center is set.

Herb Glazed Steak Kabobs

Makes 6 servings

1 (1½ lb.) boneless
   beef sirloin steak,
   cut into 1½″ pieces
2 medium red peppers,
   coarsely chopped
2 medium zucchini,
   coarsely chopped
1 large red onion,
   cut into wedges

¼ lb. whole mushrooms
½ C. mayonnaise
½ C. zesty Italian
   dressing
3 C. cooked instant
   white rice

   Preheat grill to medium high heat. Alternating, arrange steak pieces and vegetables on wooden skewers. In a medium bowl, combine mayonnaise and zesty Italian dressing. Place kabobs on grill and, using a pastry brush, brush dressing generously over kabobs. Grill kabobs for 10 to 15 minutes, turning after 8 minutes, or until steak is thoroughly cooked.

Breaded Pork Chops & Peaches

Makes 6 servings

1 (15¼ oz.) can sliced
   peaches in juice
6 (½″ thick) pork chops

2 tsp. ground ginger
1 env. pork seasoned
   coating mix

Preheat oven to 400°. Drain peaches, reserving ¼ cup syrup. Moisten pork chops with reserved peach syrup. Place seasoned coating mix in a large ziplock bag with ground ginger. Add pork chops, one or two at a time, to bag and toss until evenly coated. Place coated chops in a 10 x 15″ baking dish. Discard any remaining coating mixture. Bake for 15 minutes. Remove from oven and add sliced peaches to pan. Bake for an additional 5 minutes, or until chops are thoroughly cooked.

Swiss Beef Steak

Makes 8 servings

1 (6 lb.) chuck steak
1 (14½ oz.) can diced
   tomatoes in juice
1 (¾ oz.) env. dry onion
   soup mix
½ green pepper,
   chopped

1 (8 oz.) pkg. sliced
   mushrooms
3 T. cornstarch
2 tsp. Worcestershire
   sauce

Preheat oven to 350°. Place chuck steak in a 9 x 13″ glass baking dish. In a medium bowl, combine diced tomatoes in juice, dry onion soup mix, chopped green pepper, sliced mushrooms, cornstarch and Worcestershire sauce, mixing until well combined. Pour mixture over meat in baking dish. Cover and bake for 4 hours.

Pizza Cheeseburgers

Makes 4 servings

1 lb. ground beef
¾ tsp. garlic salt
1 (8 oz.) can pizza sauce
½ tsp. dried oregano
1 C. shredded
   mozzarella cheese

1 small onion, sliced
1 T. butter
4 hamburger buns

In a large bowl, combine ground beef and garlic salt and shape into 4 patties. In a medium saucepan over medium heat, combine pizza sauce and dried oregano. Cover and let simmer for 8 to 10 minutes, stirring occasionally. In a small skillet over medium high heat, sauté onions in butter until tender and set aside. Pan fry or grill burgers until no longer pink inside. Sprinkle shredded mozzarella cheese over burgers and heat until slightly melted. Remove burgers from heat. Spread warm pizza sauce mixture on hamburger buns and top with cheeseburgers. Top each burger with some of the sautéed onions, some of the remaining sauce and bun tops.

Slow Cooker Steak in Gravy

Makes 4 servings

1 lb. round steak,
  trimmed
1 T. vegetable oil
1¾ C. water, divided
1 (8 oz.) can tomato sauce
1 tsp. ground cumin

1¼ tsp. garlic powder
¼ tsp. salt
½ tsp. pepper
2 T. flour
4 C. hot cooked rice

Cut beef into ½″ pieces. In a large skillet over medium heat, brown beef pieces in vegetable oil. Transfer meat to a slow cooker and cover with 1½ cups water. Add tomato sauce, ground cumin, garlic powder, salt and pepper to slow cooker. Cover and cook on high setting for 4 hours, or until meat is tender. In a medium mixing bowl, combine flour and remaining ¼ cup cold water, mixing to form a paste. Stir paste into liquid in slow cooker. Cover and cook on high for an additional 35 minutes, or until gravy is thickened. Serve over hot cooked rice.

Skillet Spaghetti in Meat Sauce

Makes 6 servings

1 lb. ground beef
1 large onion, chopped
1 (7 oz.) pkg. spaghetti,
  uncooked
1 (28 oz.) can diced
  tomatoes in juice
¼ C. chopped green
  peppers
½ C. water

1 (8 oz.) can sliced
  mushrooms, drained
¾ tsp. chili powder
1 tsp. dried oregano
1 tsp. sugar
½ tsp. salt
1¼ C. shredded
  Cheddar cheese

In a large skillet over medium heat, combine ground beef and chopped onions. Cook until meat is evenly browned and onions are tender. Drain fat from skillet and stir in uncooked spaghetti, diced tomatoes in juice, chopped green peppers, water, drained mushrooms, chili powder, dried oregano, sugar and salt. Bring mixture to a boil, reduce heat, cover and let simmer for 30 to 35 minutes, or until the spaghetti is tender. Sprinkle shredded Cheddar cheese over all, cover and heat until cheese is melted.

Baked Cod Filets

Makes 8 servings

1¾ lbs. cod filets
Salt and pepper to taste
1 (10 oz.) can cream of
  mushroom soup
6 to 8 green onions,
  chopped

1 (10 oz.) can sliced
  mushrooms, drained
¼ C. milk

Preheat oven to 350°. Arrange cod filets in a single layer in a greased 9 x 13″ baking dish. Sprinkle salt and pepper over cod fillets. In a medium bowl, combine cream of mushroom soup, chopped green onions, drained sliced mushrooms and milk. Mix well and spoon mixture over fillets in baking dish. Bake, uncovered, for 20 minutes, or until fish flakes easily with a fork.

Bacon Cheddar Biscuit Casserole

Makes 8 servings

½ C. sliced
   green peppers
½ C. sliced onions
1 C. shredded
   Cheddar cheese
2 (3 oz.) boxes fully
   cooked bacon,
   crumbled

⅔ C. milk
⅛ tsp. salt
⅛ tsp. pepper
1 (12 oz.) tube
   refrigerated biscuits
3 strips bacon

Preheat oven to 350°. In a medium bowl, combine sliced green peppers, sliced onions, shredded Cheddar cheese and crumbled bacon. Toss all ingredients together. In a separate bowl combine milk, salt and pepper, mixing well. Spread green pepper mixture in an even layer across bottom of a 9 x 13″ baking dish. Pour milk mixture over ingredients in baking dish and mix lightly. Bake for 5 minutes. Separate biscuits into individual pieces and place over ingredients in baking dish. Place uncooked bacon strips across top of biscuits. Return to oven for an additional 35 minutes, or until mixture is heated and biscuits are golden brown.

Broccoli Seafood Divan

Makes 4 servings

1 (16 oz.) pkg. frozen
  broccoli, cooked
  and drained
1 lb. fresh or frozen
  white fish filets
1 (10¾ oz.) can cream
  of broccoli soup

⅓ C. milk
¼ C. shredded
  Cheddar cheese
2 T. dry bread crumbs
1 tsp. butter or
  margarine, melted
⅛ tsp. paprika

Preheat oven to 450°. In a 2 quart shallow baking dish, arrange cooked broccoli in an even layer. Top broccoli with fish filets. In a small bowl, whisk together cream of broccoli soup and milk. Pour mixture over fish and sprinkle shredded Cheddar cheese over soup mixture. In a medium bowl, toss together bread crumbs, melted butter and paprika. Sprinkle breadcrumb mixture over shredded cheese layer. Bake for 20 minutes, or until fish flakes easily with a fork.

Baked Chicken, Broccoli & Rice Dinner

Makes 6 servings

6 boneless skinless
  chicken breast halves
5 C. water, divided
2 tsp. vegetable
  bouillon granules
1¼ C. long grain white
  rice, uncooked
1 (10¾ oz.) can cream of
  chicken soup

½ C. sour cream
½ C. shredded
  Cheddar cheese
⅓ C. mayonnaise
1 tsp. curry powder
1 lb. frozen broccoli
  florets, thawed

Preheat oven to 350°. In a large saucepan over medium heat, place chicken breast halves, 2 cups water and vegetable bouillon granules. Heat for about 35 minutes, or until chicken is tender. Drain liquid from saucepan and remove from heat. Once chicken has cooled, cut chicken into cubes. In a medium saucepan, cook long grain white rice in 2½ cups water for about 20 minutes, until water has been absorbed and rice is tender. In a medium bowl, combine cream of chicken soup, sour cream, shredded Cheddar cheese, mayonnaise, curry powder and remaining ½ cup water. Mix well and spoon prepared rice into an ungreased 9 x 13″ baking dish. Cover rice with thawed broccoli and place prepared chicken over broccoli. Pour soup mixture over all. Poke holes as needed so liquid will drizzle down to bottom. Bake, uncovered, for 1 hour.

Colorado Pie

Makes 6 servings

1 (15 oz.) pkg. 9″ double
   pie crust
1 lb. ground beef
½ C. chopped onions
1 T. sugar
¼ tsp. pepper

2 (15 oz.) cans corn,
   drained
½ tsp. salt
⅛ tsp. dried oregano
1 (10¾ oz.) can
   tomato soup

Preheat oven to 400°. Prepare pastry for a double crust pie. Line a 9″ pie pan with half the pastry. Roll out top crust and set aside. In a large skillet over medium heat, cook ground beef and chopped onions until meat is evenly browned and onions are softened. Drain fat from skillet. Stir in sugar, pepper, drained corn, salt, dried oregano, and tomato soup. Mix well and pour mixture into prepared pastry lined pan. Add top crust and poke small holes for ventilation. Bake for 25 minutes.

Crispy Ranch Chicken

Makes 6 servings

2 C. ranch flavored
  potato chips, crushed
¼ tsp. pepper

6 boneless skinless
  chicken breast halves
½ C. mayonnaise

Preheat oven to 425°. In a medium bowl, combine crushed potato chips and pepper. Brush chicken breasts evenly with mayonnaise and coat generously with the crushed chips. Arrange coated chicken breast halves in a single layer on a lightly greased baking dish or baking sheet. Bake for 25 to 30 minutes, or until topping is golden brown and chicken is thoroughly cooked.

Enchilada
Squares

Makes 6 servings

1 lb. ground beef
¼ C. chopped onions
4 eggs
1 (8 oz.) can
  tomato sauce
⅔ C. evaporated milk
1½ oz. env. enchilada
  sauce mix

1 (2½ oz.) can sliced
  pitted ripe olives,
  drained
2 C. corn chips
1 C. shredded
  Cheddar cheese

In a large skillet over medium heat, cook ground beef and chopped onions until meat is browned and onions are tender. Drain off fat and spread meat mixture in an 8″ square baking dish. In a medium bowl, beat together eggs, tomato sauce, evaporated milk and enchilada sauce mix. Pour mixture over meat in baking dish sprinkle sliced olives and corn chips over top. Bake, uncovered, for 20 to 25 minutes, or until center is set. Remove from oven and sprinkle shredded Cheddar cheese over all. Return to oven for an additional 3 to 5 minutes, or until cheese is melted.

Creamy Hash Brown Casserole

Makes 8 servings

1 (10¾ oz.) can cream
of potato soup
¼ C. butter or margarine
2 C. sour cream
1 (2 lb.) pkg. frozen hash
brown potatoes,
thawed

⅓ C. chopped
green onions
2 C. shredded Cheddar
cheese, divided
Salt and pepper to taste

Preheat oven to 350°. In a small saucepan over low heat, combine cream of potato soup, butter and sour cream. Cook, stirring occasionally, until butter and sour cream are completely melted. In a large bowl, combine hash brown potatoes, chopped green onions and 1 cup shredded Cheddar cheese. Add heated soup mixture. Mix well and season with salt and pepper to taste. Transfer mixture to a 9 x 13″ baking dish. Sprinkle remaining 1 cup shredded Cheddar cheese over top. Bake for 30 to 45 minutes. Remove from oven and serve warm.

Sour Cream
& Chive Potato
Chicken Bake

1 pkg. instant sour
   cream and chive
   flavored mashed
   potatoes
2 (12½ oz.) cans cooked
   chunk chicken

1 T. butter or margarine
1 T. flour
½ C. chicken broth
1 T. heavy cream
1 C. shredded Colby Jack
   cheese blend

Preheat oven to 375°. Prepare mashed potatoes according to package directions and spread cooked mashed potatoes evenly across bottom of a 9 x 13″ baking dish. Top with drained cooked chunk chicken. In a medium saucepan over medium heat, melt butter. Mix in flour, chicken broth and heavy cream. Heat, stirring occasionally, until mixture has thickened. Pour mixture over potatoes and chicken in baking dish. Top with shredded Colby Jack cheese blend. Bake, uncovered, for 25 minutes.

Chunky Chicken & Rice Soup

Makes 5 cups

½ lb. boneless skinless
   chicken breasts, cubed
1 (10¾ oz.) can
   chicken broth
1½ C. water
1 (10 oz.) pkg. frozen
   mixed vegetables,
   thawed

1 env. Italian salad
   dressing mix
½ C. white rice,
   uncooked

Grease a large soup pot with non-stick cooking spray. Add cubed chicken and cook, stirring occasionally, for 8 minutes or until chicken is no longer pink. Stir in chicken broth, water, mixed vegetables and salad dressing mix. Bring mixture to a boil, reduce heat to low, cover and let simmer for 5 minutes, or until vegetables are tender. Stir in uncooked white rice. Cover and simmer for an additional 20 minutes. Remove from heat. Let stand 5 minutes before serving.

Hot Turkey Sandwiches

Makes 4 servings

1 (6 oz.) pkg. stuffing mix
1 (10½ oz.) can
   chicken gravy

4 slices bread
3 (6 oz.) pkgs. deli
   sliced turkey

Prepare stuffing mix according to package directions and set aside. In a small saucepan over medium heat, cook chicken gravy until heated throughout and smooth. Arrange one slice of bread on each of four plates. Divide turkey slices onto each piece of bread. Top turkey on each sandwich with ¾ cup of the hot prepared stuffing. Pour ¼ cup gravy over each sandwich. Serve immediately.

Favorite Tuna Casserole

Makes 4 to 6 servings

¾ lb. processed cheese food, cubed
⅔ C. milk
1 (3 oz.) pkg. cream cheese, cubed
3 C. medium noodles, cooked and drained

1 (10 oz.) pkg. frozen peas, thawed
1 (6 oz.) can tuna, drained
1 C. crushed potato chips

Preheat oven to 350°. In a large saucepan over low heat, combine cubed cheese, milk and cubed cream cheese. Heat, stirring frequently, until mixture is completely melted. Stir in cooked noodles, thawed peas and tuna. Mix well and spoon mixture in to a 2-quart casserole dish. Sprinkle crushed potato chips over top. Bake for 20 to 25 minutes, or until casserole is heated throughout.

Index

My Favorite Recipes

Title	Page #
_____	_____
_____	_____
_____	_____
_____	_____
_____	_____
_____	_____
_____	_____
_____	_____
_____	_____
_____	_____
_____	_____
_____	_____
_____	_____
_____	_____
_____	_____
_____	_____
_____	_____
_____	_____